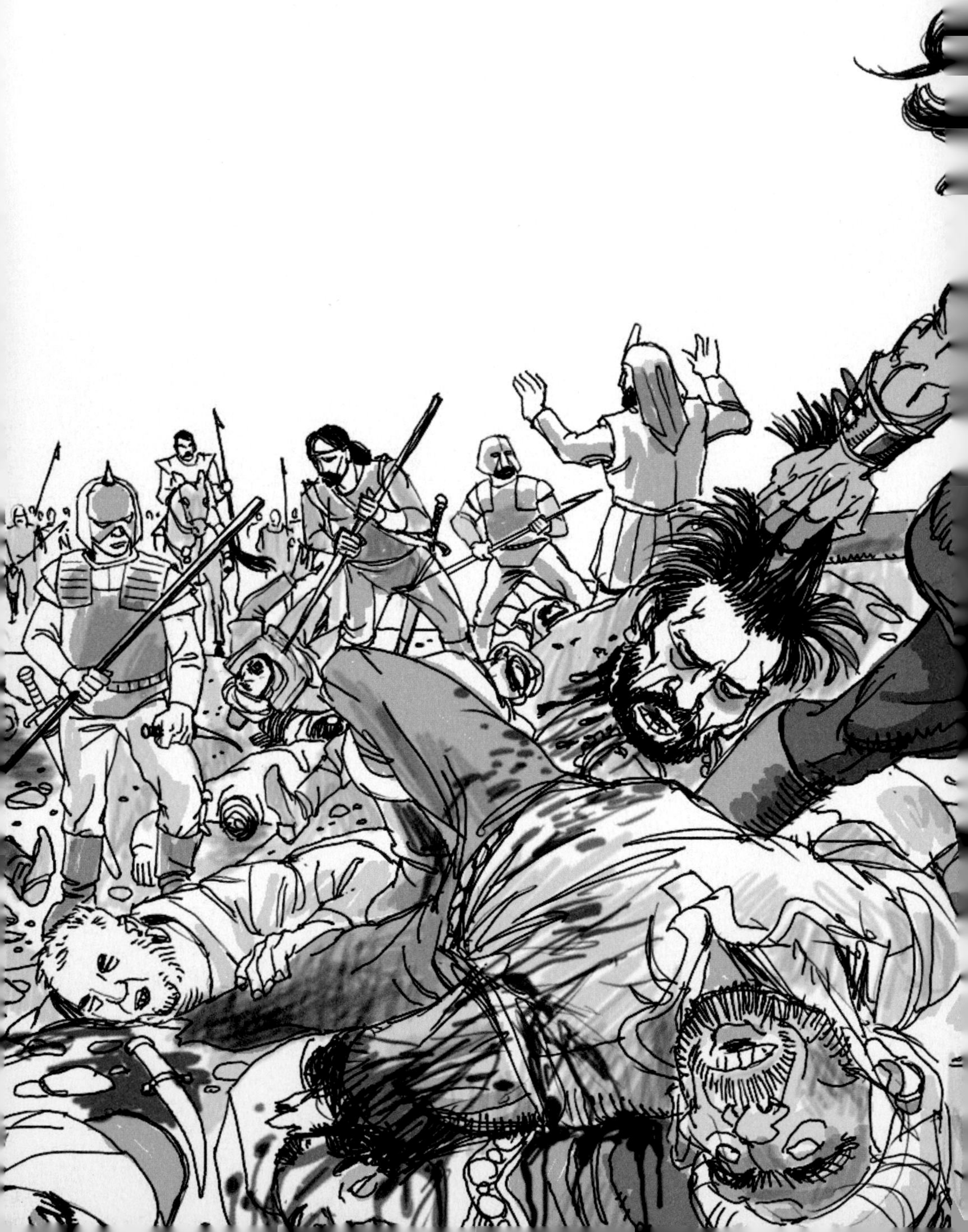

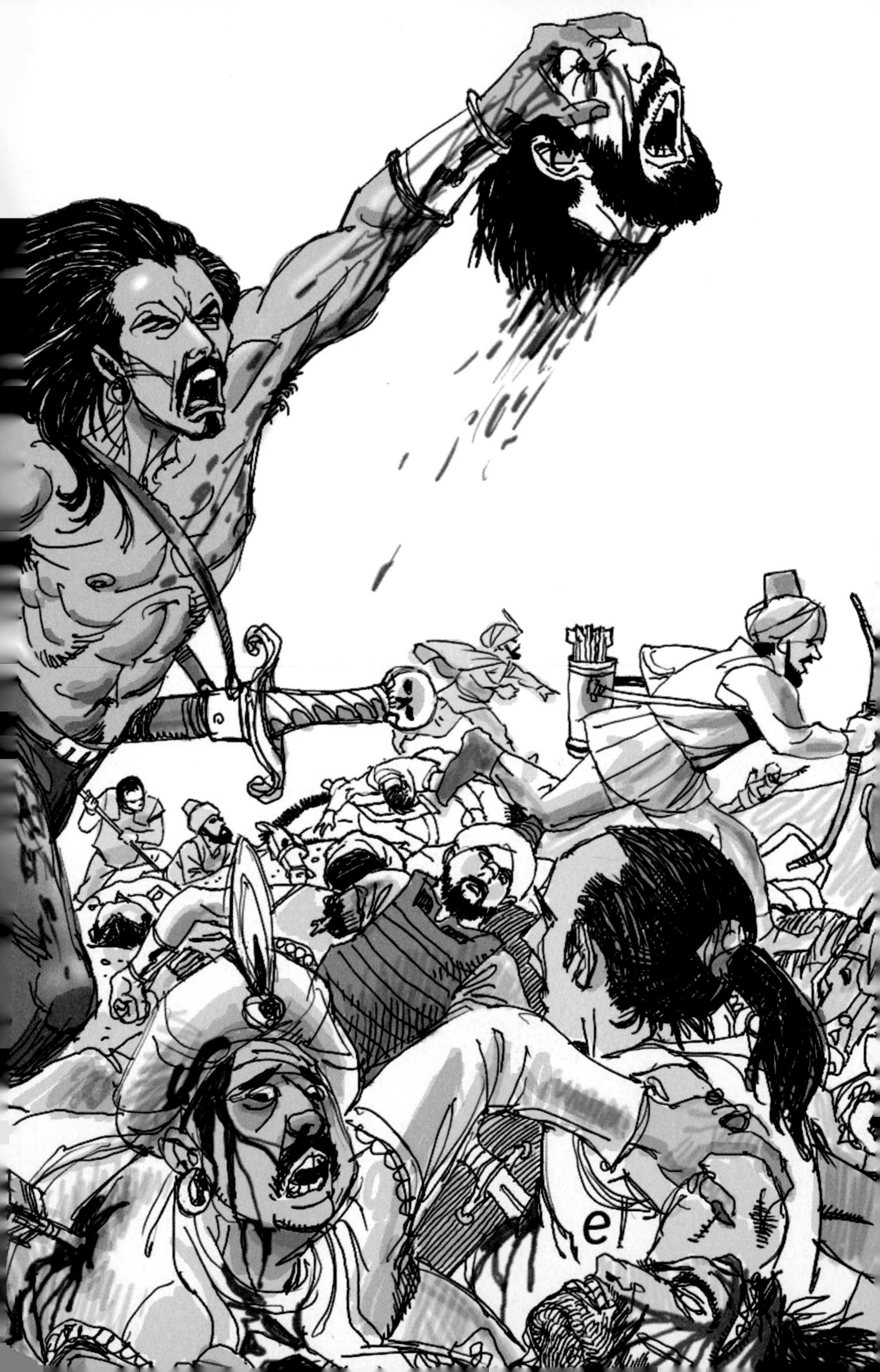
e

VLAD THE IMPALER

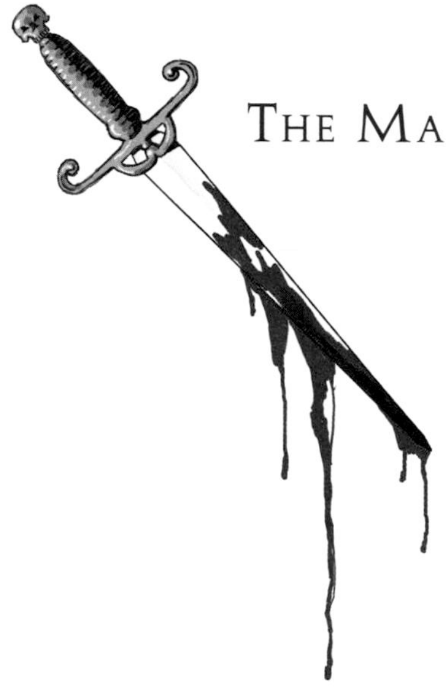

The Man Who Was Dracula

SID JACOBSON and ERNIE COLÓN

Hudson Street Press

HUDSON STREET PRESS
Published by Penguin Group
Penguin Group (USA) Inc., 375 Hudson Street, New York, New York 10014, U.S.A.
Penguin Group (Canada), 90 Eglinton Avenue East, Suite 700, Toronto, Ontario, Canada M4P 2Y3 (a division of Pearson Penguin Canada Inc.)
Penguin Books Ltd., 80 Strand, London WC2R 0RL, England
Penguin Ireland, 25 St. Stephen's Green, Dublin 2, Ireland (a division of Penguin Books Ltd.)
Penguin Group (Australia), 250 Camberwell Road, Camberwell, Victoria 3124, Australia (a division of Pearson Australia Group Pty. Ltd.)
Penguin Books India Pvt. Ltd., 11 Community Centre, Panchsheel Park, New Delhi – 110 017, India
Penguin Books (NZ), cnr Airborne and Rosedale Roads, Albany, Auckland 1310, New Zealand (a division of Pearson New Zealand Ltd.)
Penguin Books (South Africa) (Pty.) Ltd., 24 Sturdee Avenue, Rosebank, Johannesburg 2196, South Africa

Penguin Books Ltd., Registered Offices: 80 Strand, London WC2R 0RL, England

First published by Hudson Street Press, a member of Penguin Group (USA) Inc.

First Printing, October 2009
1   3   5   7   9   10   8   6   4   2

Text Copyright © Sid Jacobson, 2009
Illustrations Copyright © Ernie Colón, 2009
All rights reserved

REGISTERED TRADEMARK—MARCA REGISTRADA

HUDSON
STREET
PRESS

LIBRARY OF CONGRESS CATALOGING-IN-PUBLICATION DATA

Jacobson, Sidney.
Vlad the Impaler : the man who was Dracula / Sid Jacobson and Ernie Colón.
p. cm.
ISBN 978-1-59463-058-3 (alk. paper)
1. Vlad III, Prince of Wallachia, 1430 or 31-1476 or 7--Comic books, strips, etc. 2. Graphic novels. I. Colón, Ernie. II. Title.
PN6727.J35V56 2009
741.5'973--dc22
2009028610

Printed in the United States of America

PUBLISHER'S NOTE
This is a work of fiction. Names, characters, places, and incidents are either the product of the authors' imagination or are used fictitiously, and any resemblance to actual persons, living or dead, business establishments, events, or locales is entirely coincidental.

BOOKS ARE AVAILABLE AT QUANTITY DISCOUNTS WHEN USED TO PROMOTE PRODUCTS OR SERVICES. FOR INFORMATION PLEASE WRITE TO PREMIUM MARKETING DIVISION, PENGUIN GROUP (USA) INC., 375 HUDSON STREET, NEW YORK, NEW YORK 10014.

Unlike the protagonist of the story you are about to read,

we gratefully dedicate this book to our respective wives,

Ruth Ashby Colón and Shure Jacobson,

for their patience and their unqualified love.

ACKNOWLEDGMENTS

We would like to thank and acknowledge the thoughtful and precise aid we received in the layout art by Francesco Guerrini (Alcadia SRC), Italy; the sympathetic, intelligent, and consistent polishing by our editor, Anna Sternoff, who took an "orphaned" book and made it one of her very own; and to our agent, Lydia Wills, who keeps leading us to places we never dreamed we'd be. We would also like to thank Lavina Lee, Matthew Boezi, Amy Hill, Alissa Amell, and Jason Johnson for their special help and skills in bringing this book to completion in the face of the demons of time.

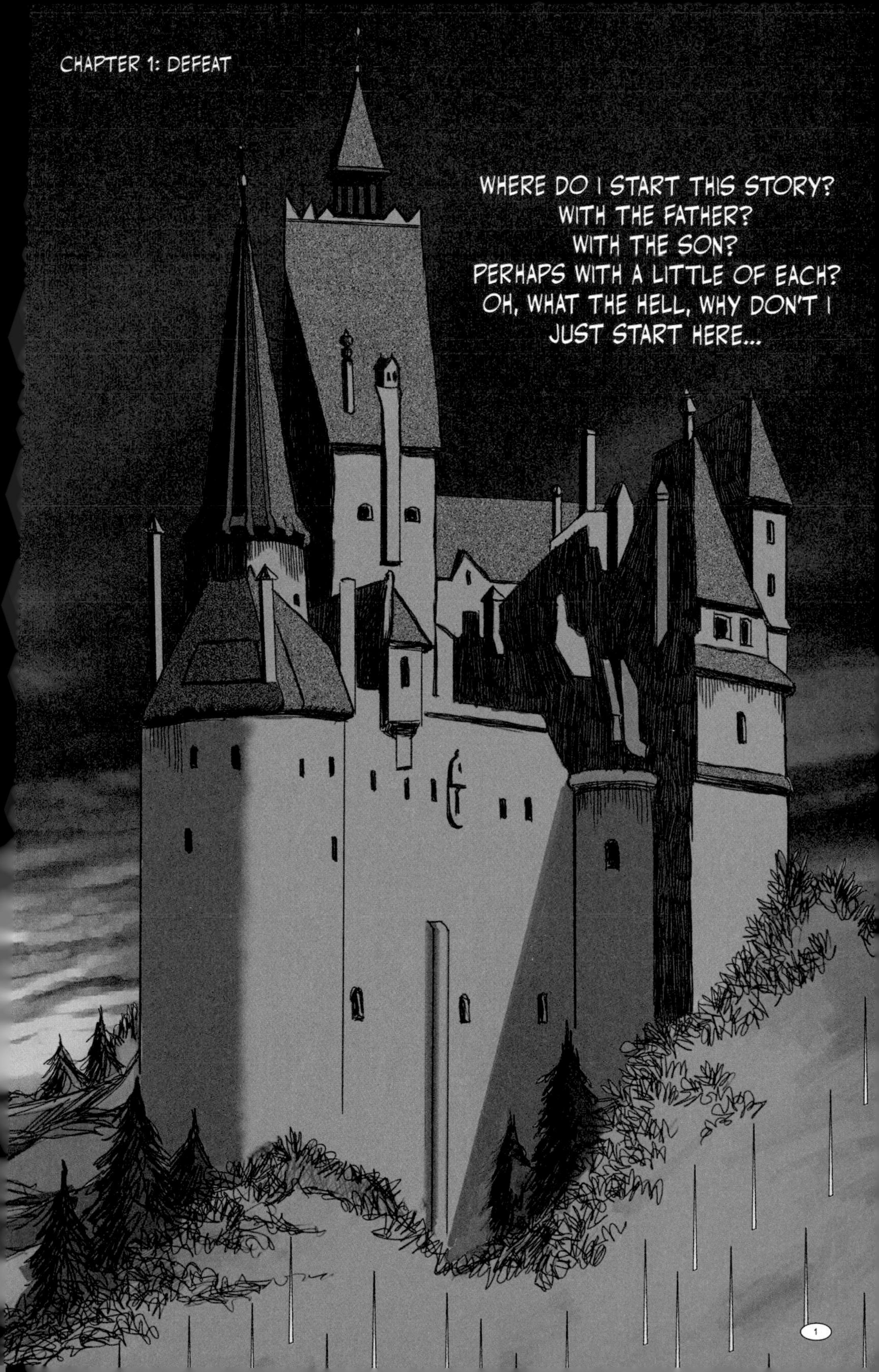
CHAPTER 1: DEFEAT
WHERE DO I START THIS STORY?
WITH THE FATHER?
WITH THE SON?
PERHAPS WITH A LITTLE OF EACH?
OH, WHAT THE HELL, WHY DON'T I
JUST START HERE...

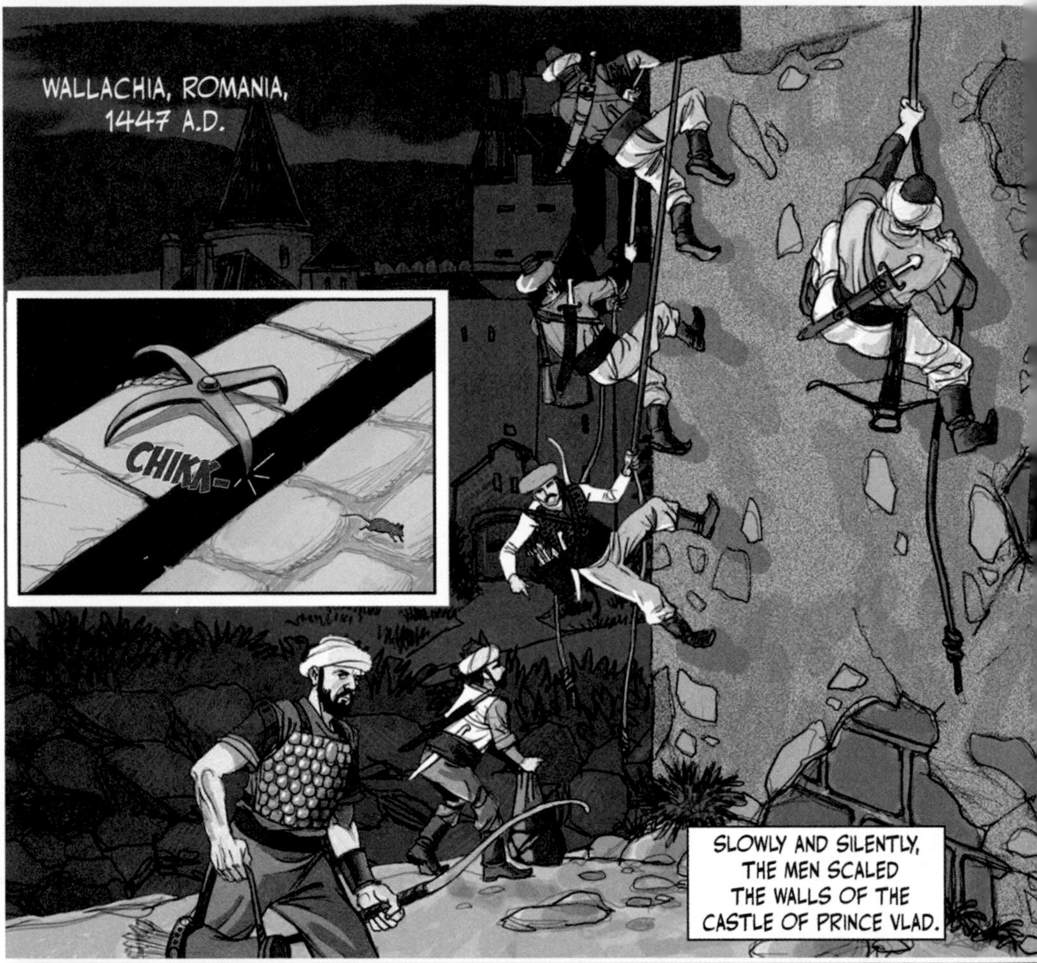
WALLACHIA, ROMANIA, 1447 A.D.
CHIKK-
SLOWLY AND SILENTLY, THE MEN SCALED THE WALLS OF THE CASTLE OF PRINCE VLAD.

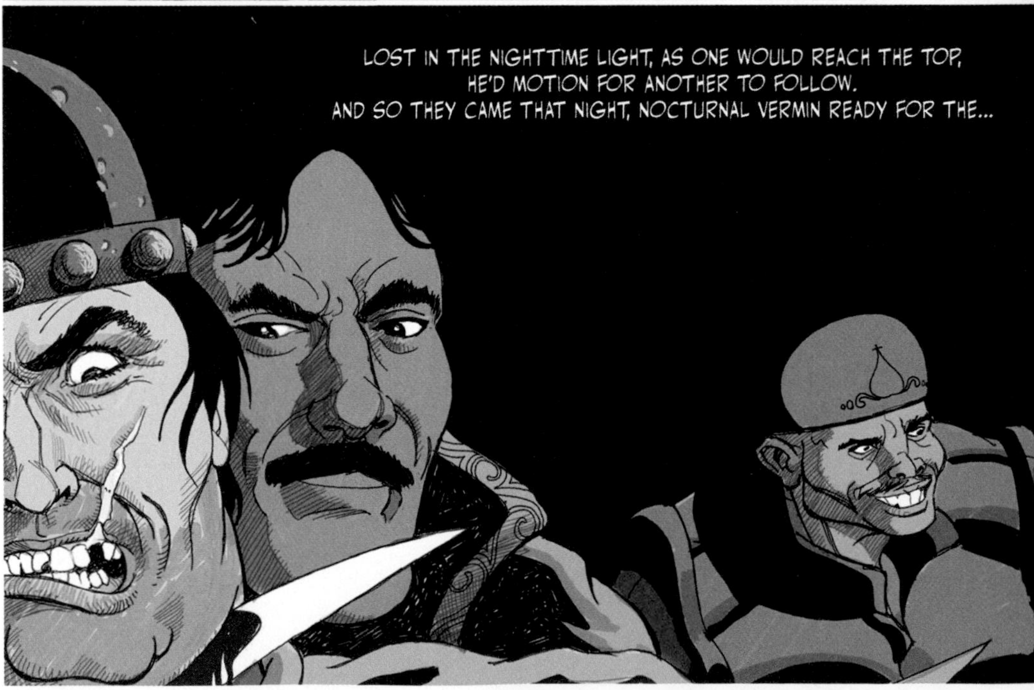
LOST IN THE NIGHTTIME LIGHT, AS ONE WOULD REACH THE TOP, HE'D MOTION FOR ANOTHER TO FOLLOW. AND SO THEY CAME THAT NIGHT, NOCTURNAL VERMIN READY FOR THE...

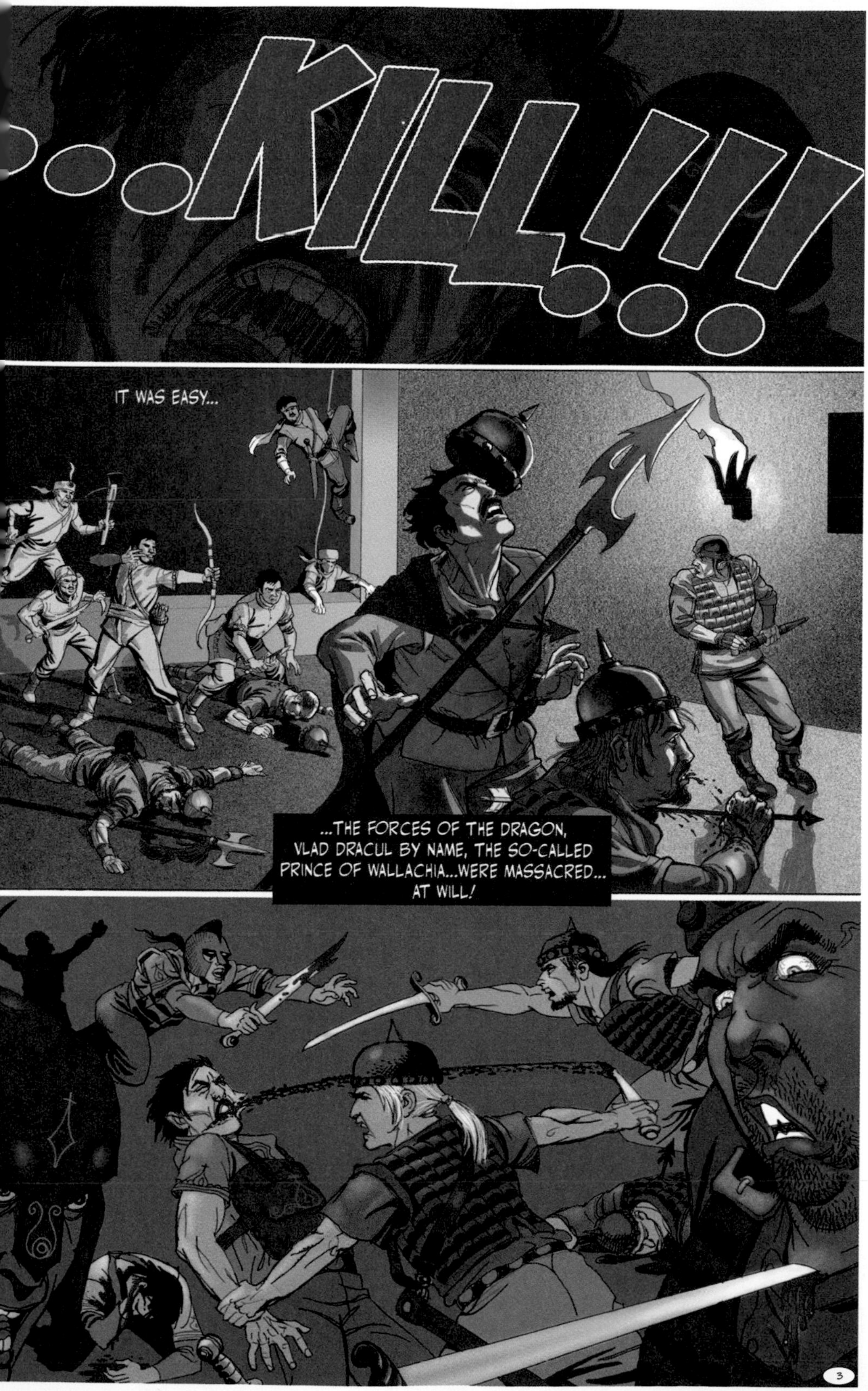
...KILL!!!!...
IT WAS EASY...
...THE FORCES OF THE DRAGON, VLAD DRACUL BY NAME, THE SO-CALLED PRINCE OF WALLACHIA...WERE MASSACRED... AT WILL!

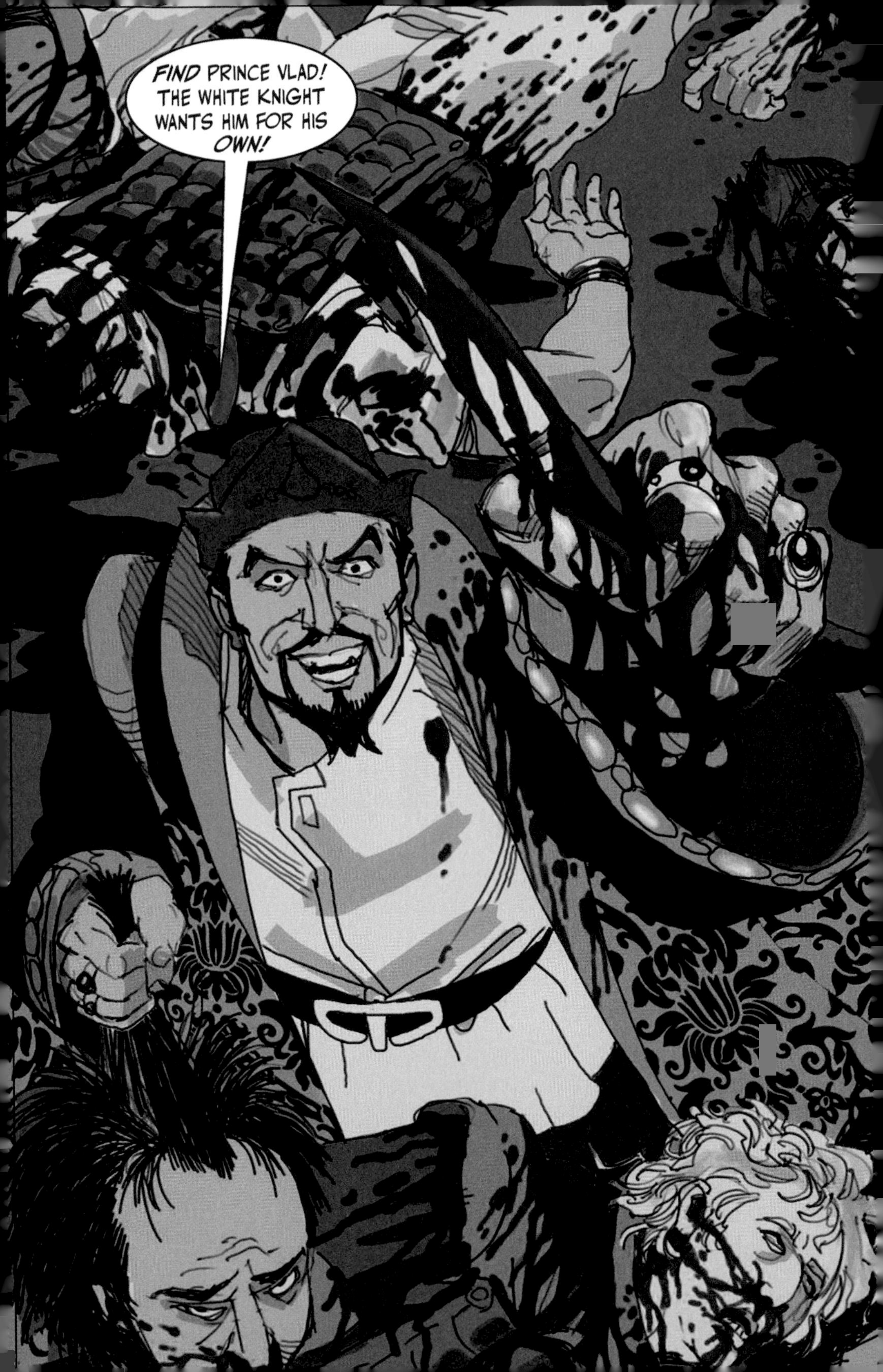
FIND PRINCE VLAD! THE WHITE KNIGHT WANTS HIM FOR HIS OWN!

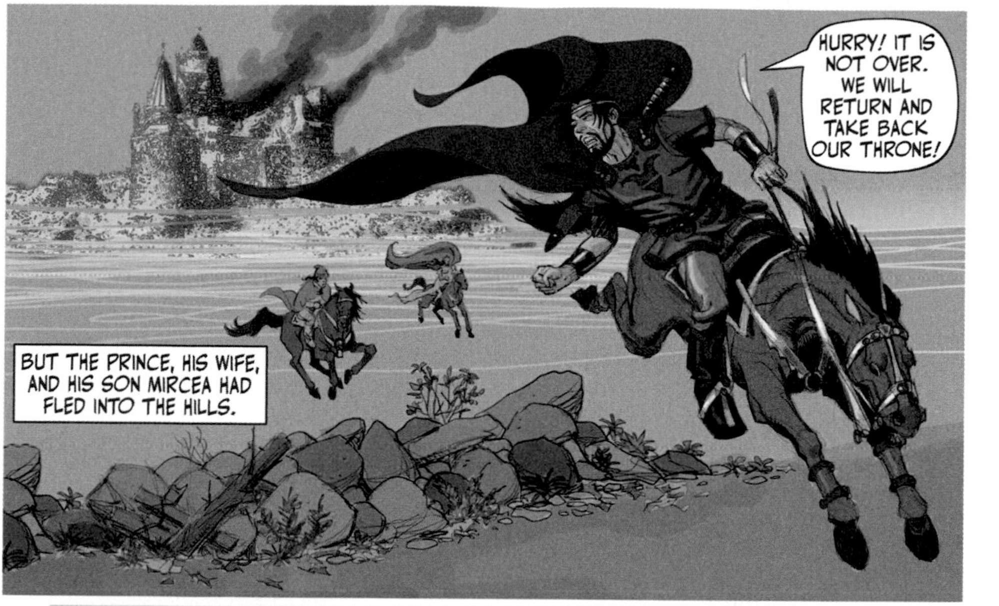
HURRY! IT IS NOT OVER. WE WILL RETURN AND TAKE BACK OUR THRONE!
BUT THE PRINCE, HIS WIFE, AND HIS SON MIRCEA HAD FLED INTO THE HILLS.

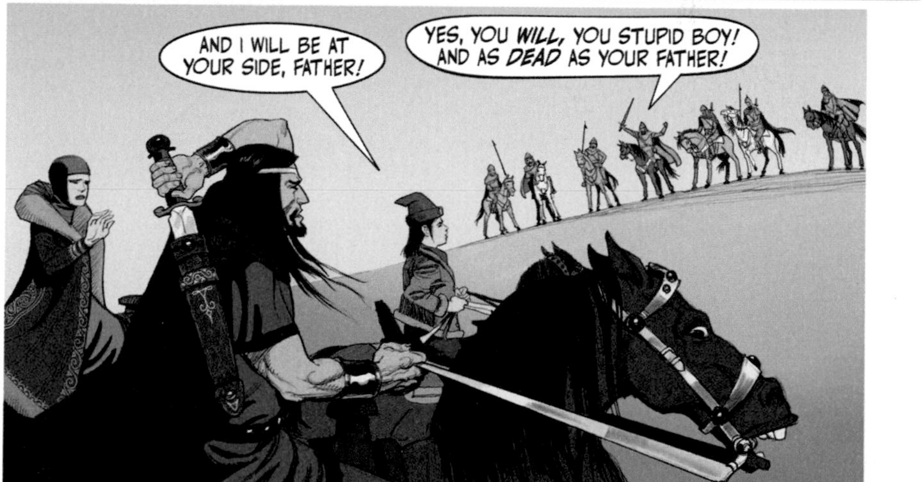
AND I WILL BE AT YOUR SIDE, FATHER!
YES, YOU WILL, YOU STUPID BOY! AND AS DEAD AS YOUR FATHER!

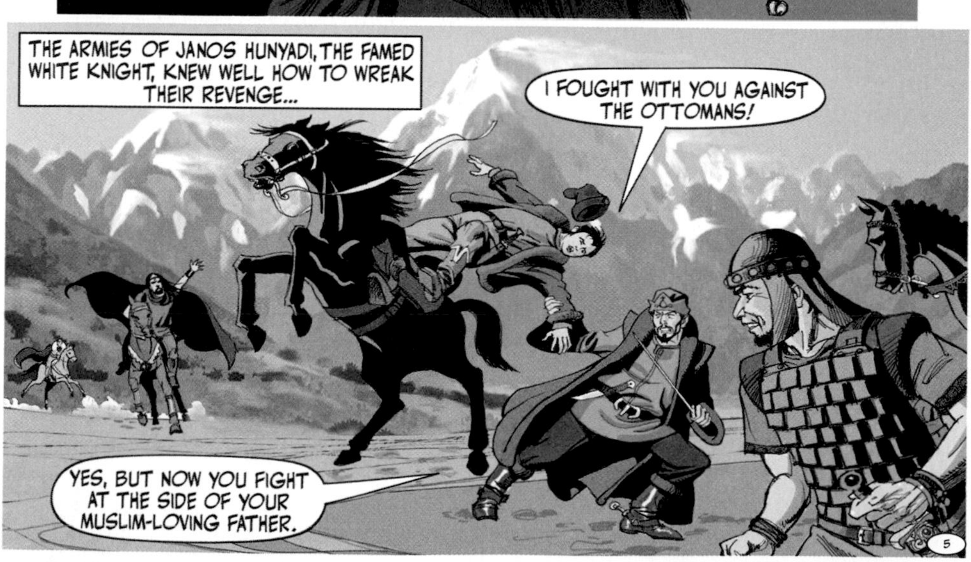
THE ARMIES OF JANOS HUNYADI, THE FAMED WHITE KNIGHT, KNEW WELL HOW TO WREAK THEIR REVENGE...
I FOUGHT WITH YOU AGAINST THE OTTOMANS!
YES, BUT NOW YOU FIGHT AT THE SIDE OF YOUR MUSLIM-LOVING FATHER.

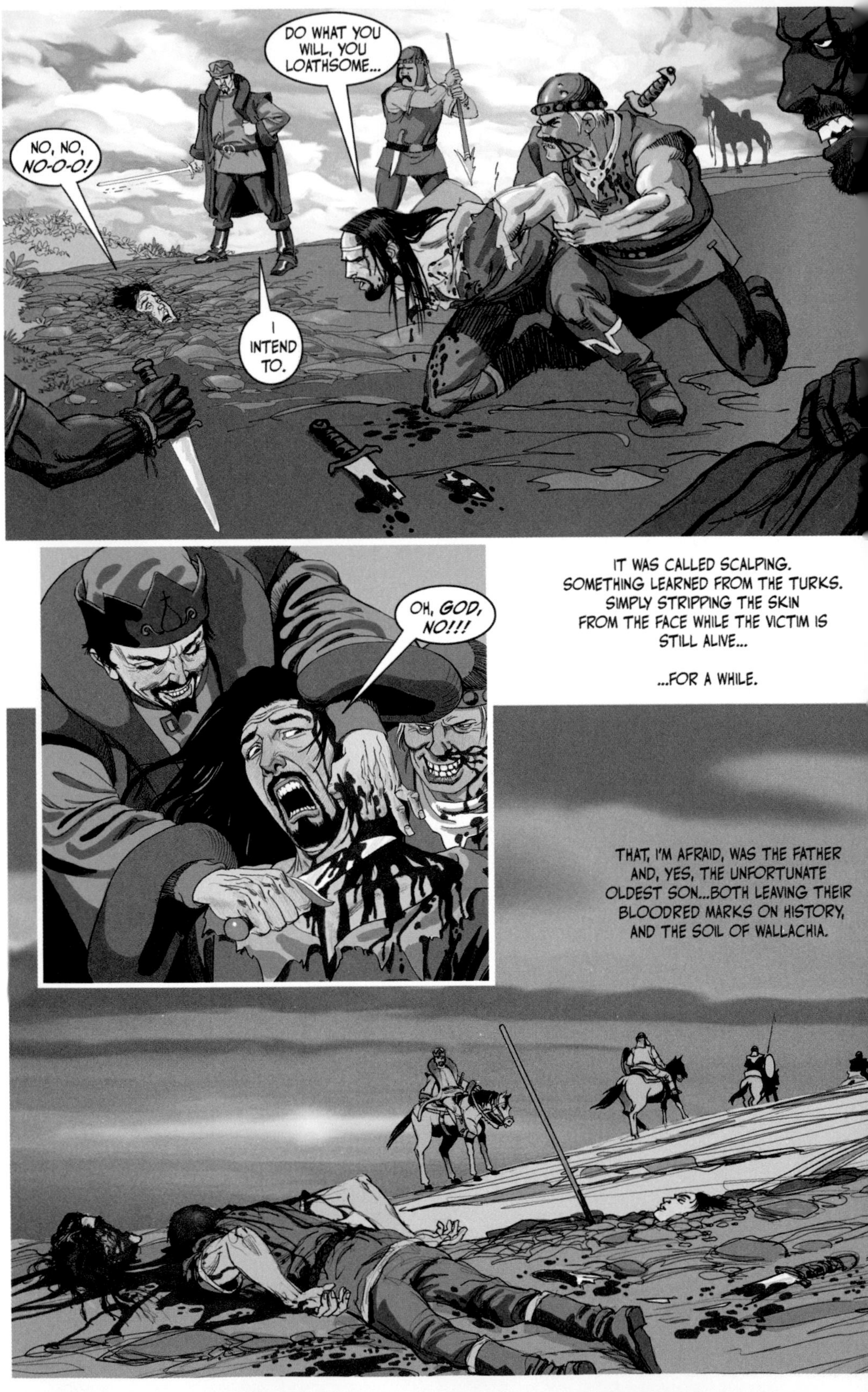
NO, NO, NO-O-O!
DO WHAT YOU WILL, YOU LOATHSOME...
I INTEND TO.
IT WAS CALLED SCALPING. SOMETHING LEARNED FROM THE TURKS. SIMPLY STRIPPING THE SKIN FROM THE FACE WHILE THE VICTIM IS STILL ALIVE...
...FOR A WHILE.
OH, GOD, NO!!!
THAT, I'M AFRAID, WAS THE FATHER AND, YES, THE UNFORTUNATE OLDEST SON...BOTH LEAVING THEIR BLOODRED MARKS ON HISTORY, AND THE SOIL OF WALLACHIA.

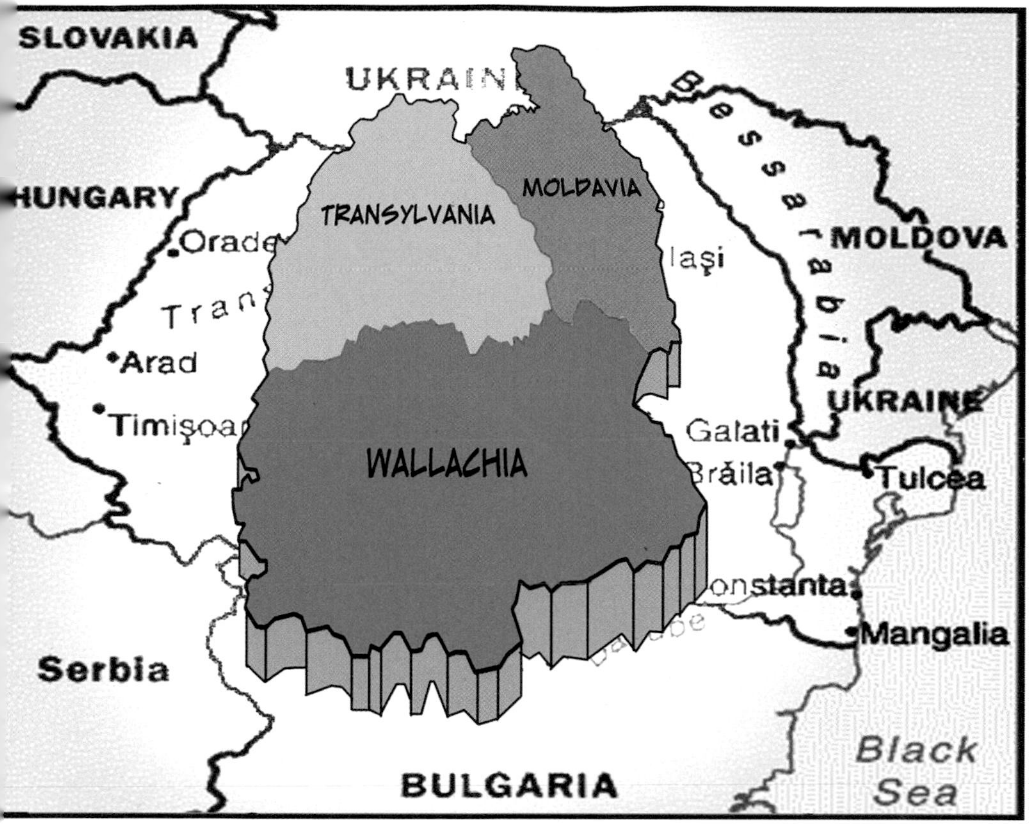
SLOVAKIA
UKRAIN
HUNGARY
TRANSYLVANIA
MOLDAVIA
Bessarabia
MOLDOVA
Orade
Iaşi
Tran
Arad
Timişoar
UKRAINE
Galati
WALLACHIA
Brăila
Tulcea
onstanta
Mangalia
Serbia
Black Sea
BULGARIA

BUT WHAT THE HELL, YOU MAY ASK.
IS THIS WALLACHIA? AND WHAT KIND OF HISTORY AM I TALKING ABOUT? ALONG WITH MOLDAVIA AND TRANSYLVANIA, WALLACHIA WAS AND IS PART OF ROMANIA.

BACK IN THE 1400'S, WALLACHIA WAS A PRINCIPALITY.
THOUGH IT WAS GOVERNED BY ITS OWN PRINCES, THE OTTOMAN EMPIRE EXERCISED POLITICAL CONTROL OVER THE AREA AND TRIBUTES WERE PAID TO THE TURKISH SULTAN.
MOST TROUBLES CAME FROM CHRISTIAN PRINCES WARRING EACH OTHER FOR THE CROWN--JUST LIKE YOU WITNESSED BETWEEN PRINCE VLAD II AND THE WHITE KNIGHT. THE MUSLIMS, IN THEIR OWN WAY, WERE PUSSYCATS.

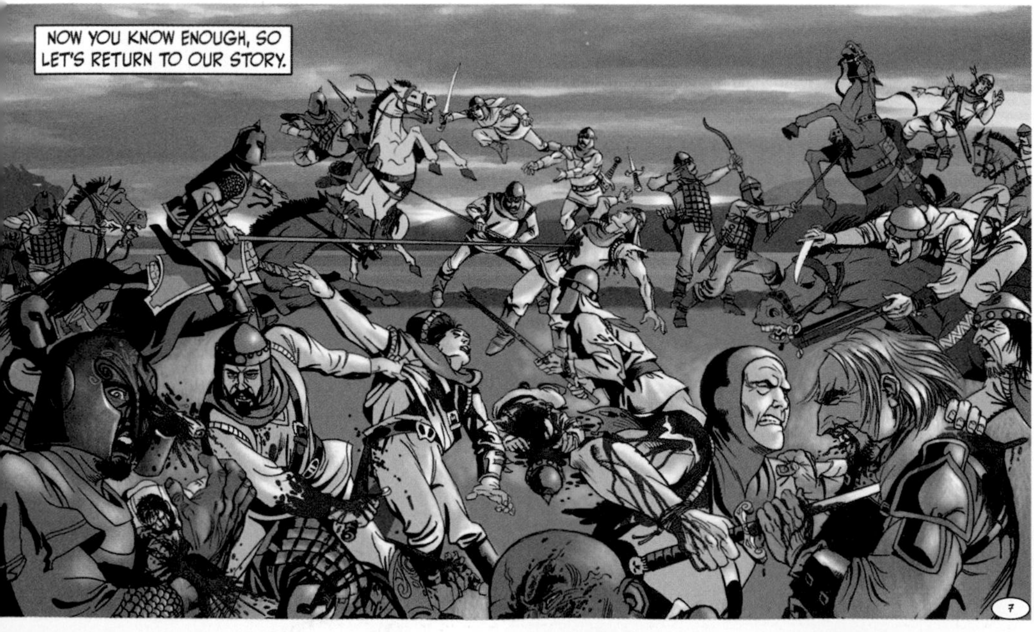
NOW YOU KNOW ENOUGH, SO LET'S RETURN TO OUR STORY.

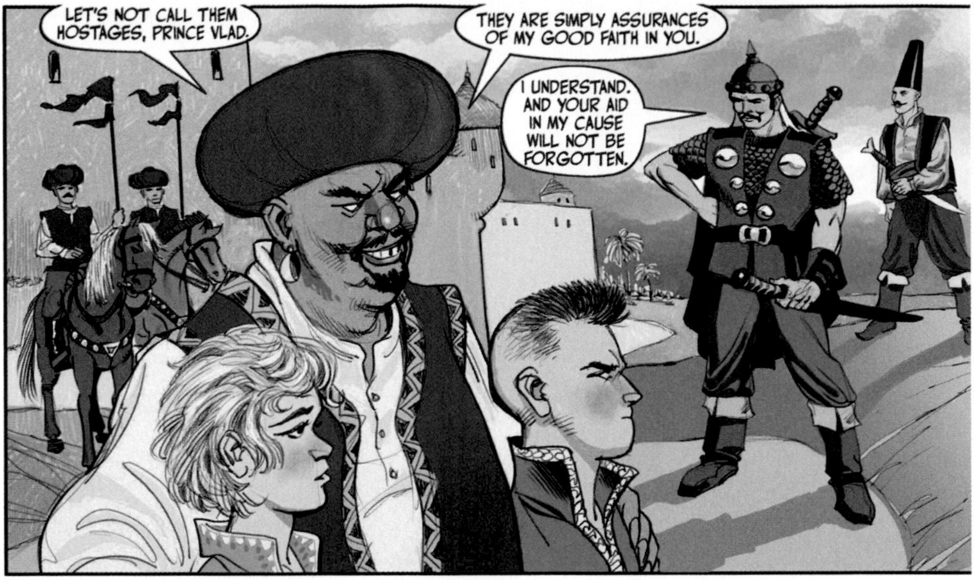
LET'S NOT CALL THEM HOSTAGES, PRINCE VLAD.
THEY ARE SIMPLY ASSURANCES OF MY GOOD FAITH IN YOU.
I UNDERSTAND. AND YOUR AID IN MY CAUSE WILL NOT BE FORGOTTEN.

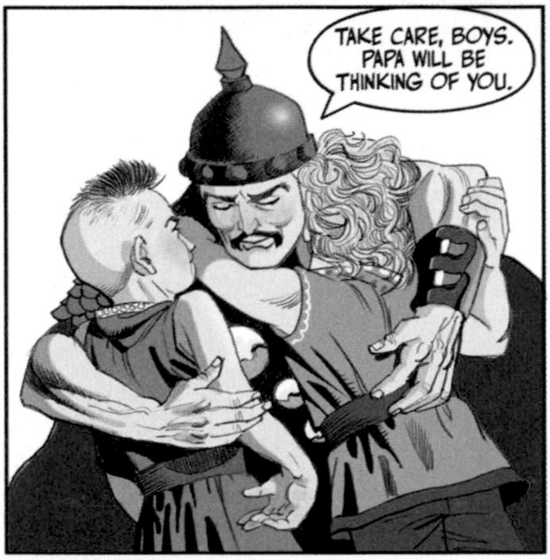
TAKE CARE, BOYS. PAPA WILL BE THINKING OF YOU.

AS YOU MIGHT NOT KNOW, THERE WERE TWO OTHER SONS. SEVERAL YEARS EARLIER THEY WERE LEFT IN THE HANDS OF SULTAN MURAD OF THE OTTOMAN EMPIRE, IN ADRIANOPLE, IN EASTERN EUROPEAN TURKEY.

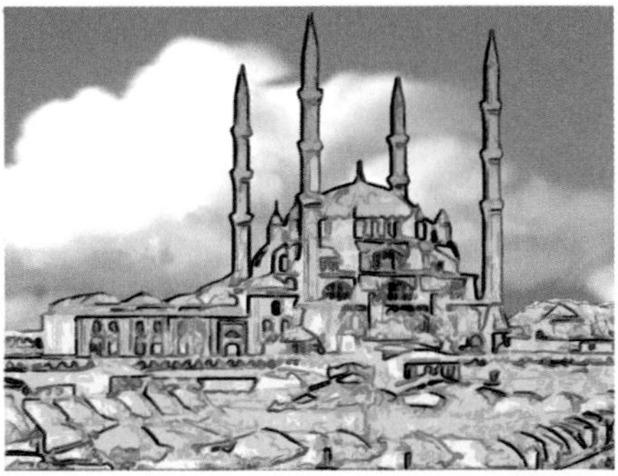

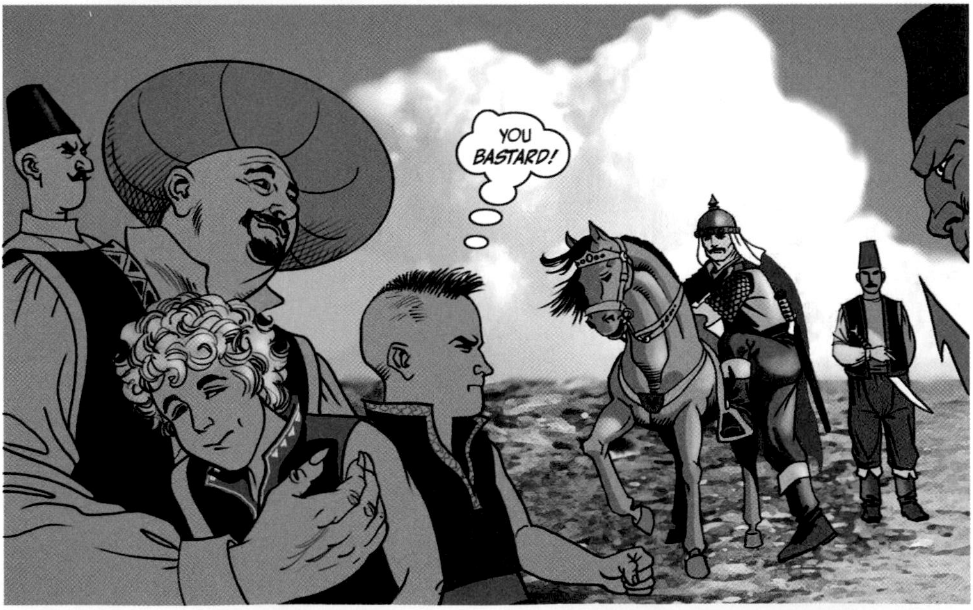
YOU *BASTARD!*

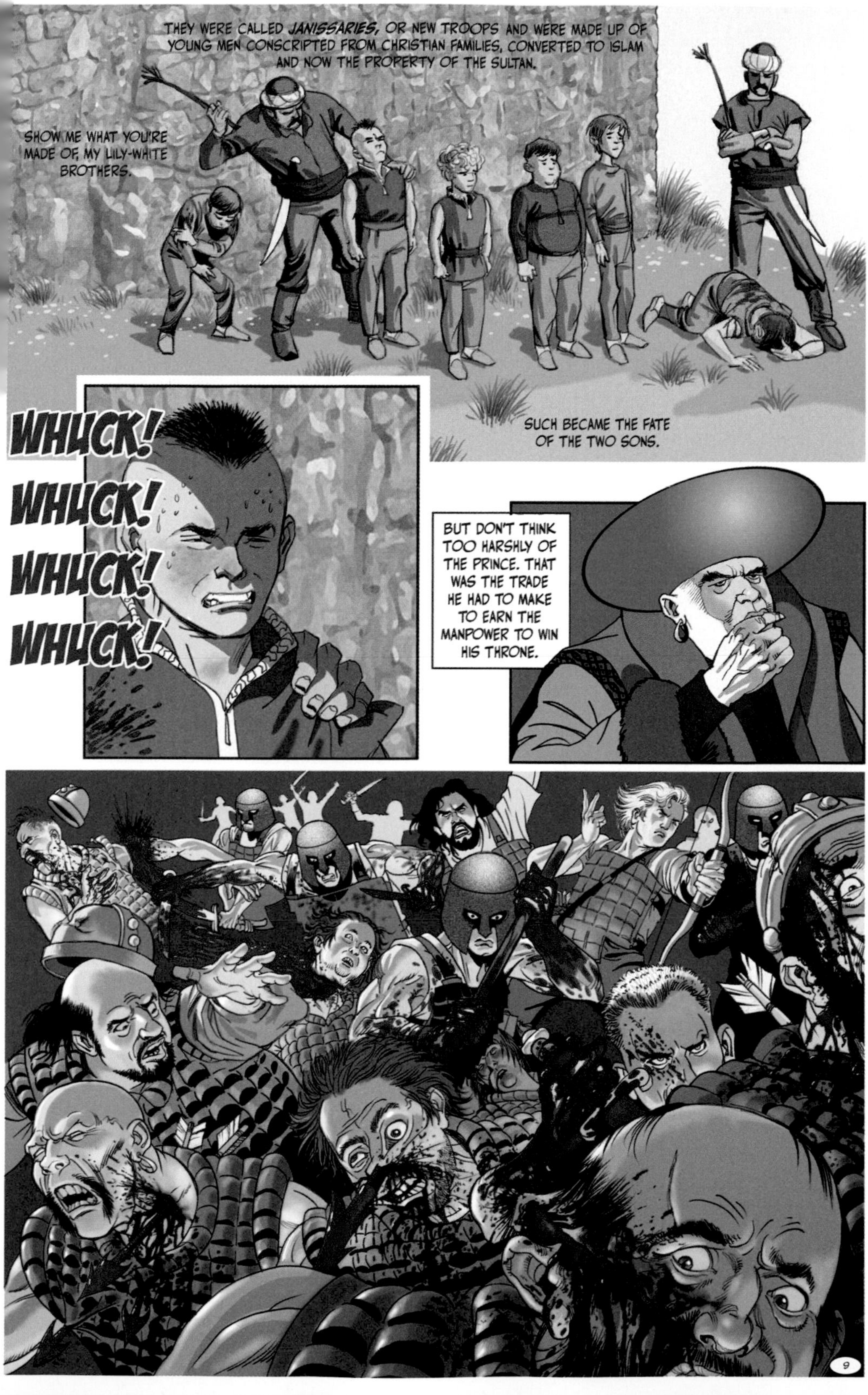
THEY WERE CALLED *JANISSARIES,* OR NEW TROOPS AND WERE MADE UP OF YOUNG MEN CONSCRIPTED FROM CHRISTIAN FAMILIES, CONVERTED TO ISLAM AND NOW THE PROPERTY OF THE SULTAN.
SHOW ME WHAT YOU'RE MADE OF, MY LILY-WHITE BROTHERS.
SUCH BECAME THE FATE OF THE TWO SONS.
WHUCK! WHUCK! WHUCK! WHUCK!
BUT DON'T THINK TOO HARSHLY OF THE PRINCE. THAT WAS THE TRADE HE HAD TO MAKE TO EARN THE MANPOWER TO WIN HIS THRONE.

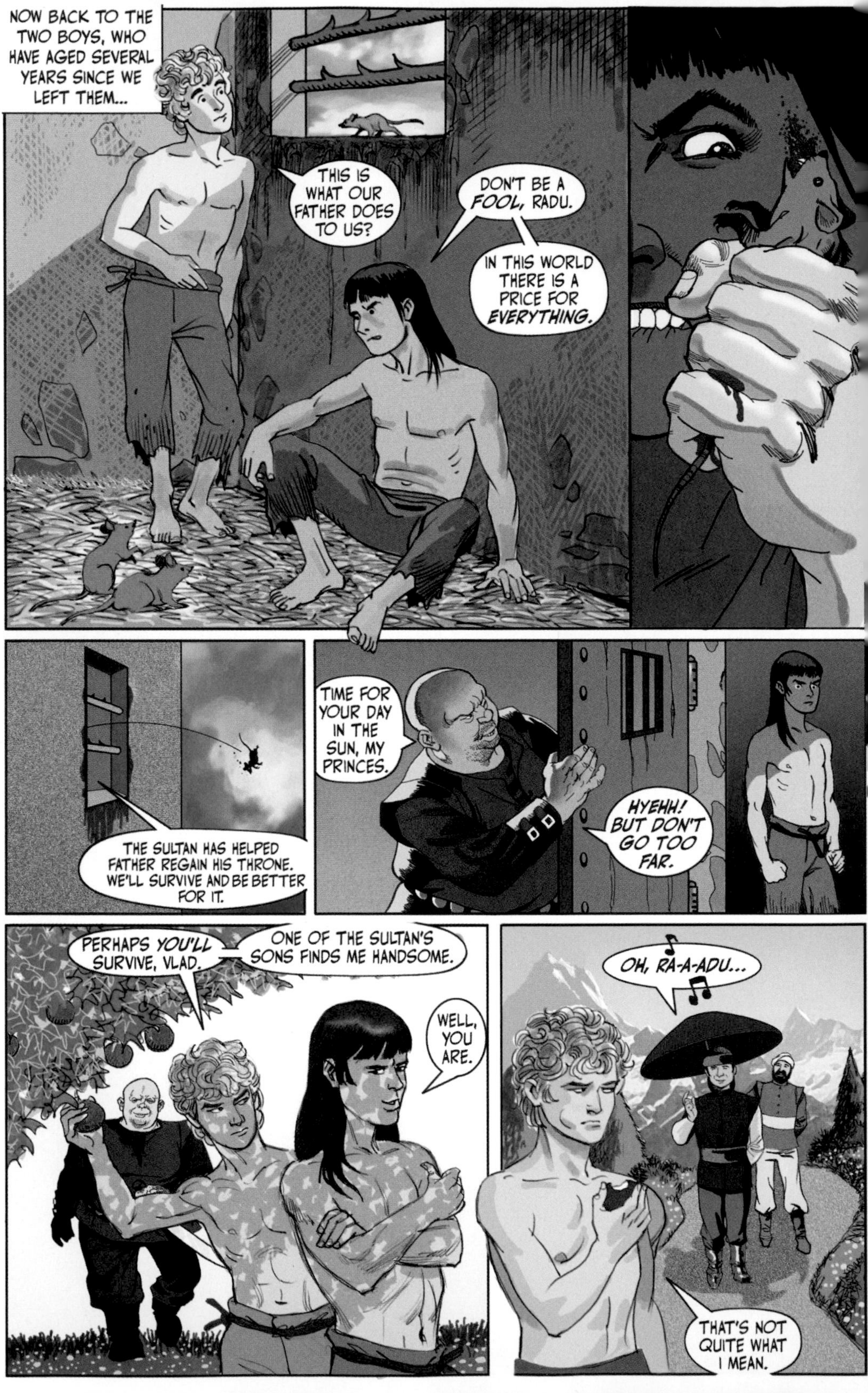
NOW BACK TO THE TWO BOYS, WHO HAVE AGED SEVERAL YEARS SINCE WE LEFT THEM...
THIS IS WHAT OUR FATHER DOES TO US?
DON'T BE A *FOOL,* RADU.
IN THIS WORLD THERE IS A PRICE FOR *EVERYTHING.*
THE SULTAN HAS HELPED FATHER REGAIN HIS THRONE. WE'LL SURVIVE AND BE BETTER FOR IT.
TIME FOR YOUR DAY IN THE SUN, MY PRINCES.
HYEHH! BUT DON'T GO TOO FAR.
PERHAPS *YOU'LL* SURVIVE, VLAD.
ONE OF THE SULTAN'S SONS FINDS ME HANDSOME.
WELL, YOU ARE.
OH, RA-A-ADU...
THAT'S NOT QUITE WHAT I MEAN.

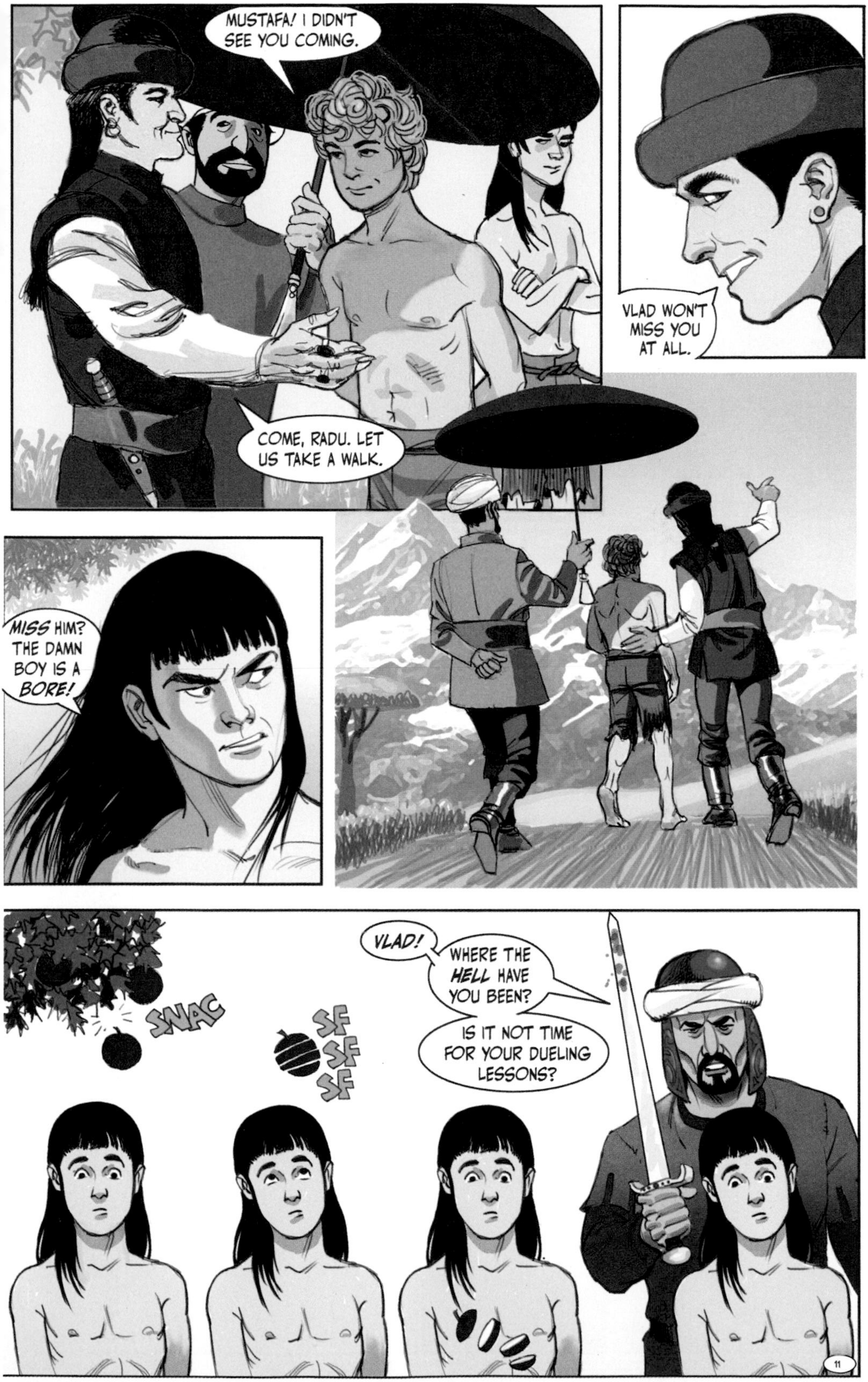
MUSTAFA! I DIDN'T SEE YOU COMING.
VLAD WON'T MISS YOU AT ALL.
COME, RADU. LET US TAKE A WALK.
MISS HIM? THE DAMN BOY IS A BORE!
SNAC
SF SF SF
VLAD!
WHERE THE HELL HAVE YOU BEEN?
IS IT NOT TIME FOR YOUR DUELING LESSONS?

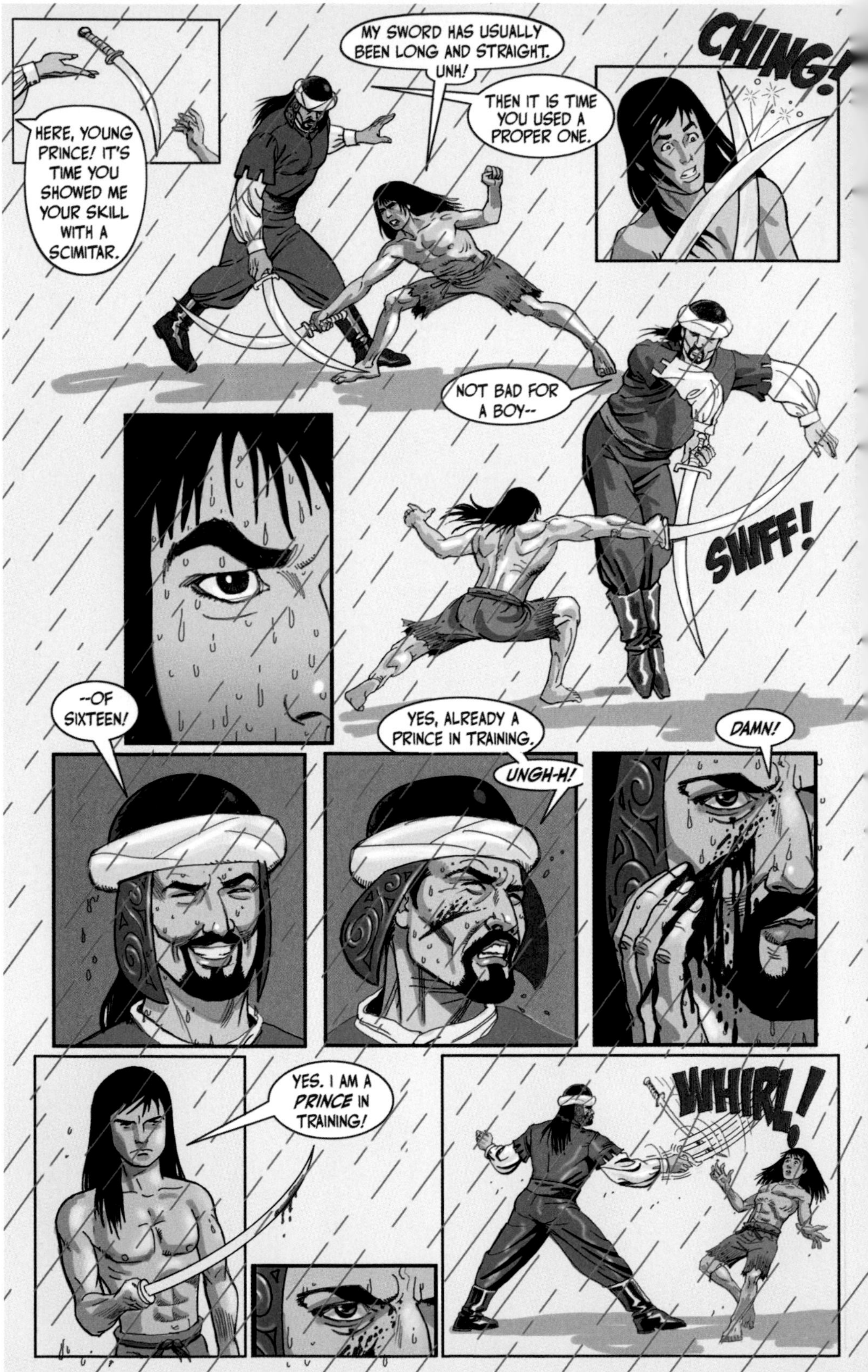
HERE, YOUNG PRINCE! IT'S TIME YOU SHOWED ME YOUR SKILL WITH A SCIMITAR.
MY SWORD HAS USUALLY BEEN LONG AND STRAIGHT. UNH!
THEN IT IS TIME YOU USED A PROPER ONE.
CHING!
NOT BAD FOR A BOY--
SWFF!
--OF SIXTEEN!
YES, ALREADY A PRINCE IN TRAINING.
UNGH-H!
DAMN!
YES. I AM A *PRINCE* IN TRAINING!
WHIRL!

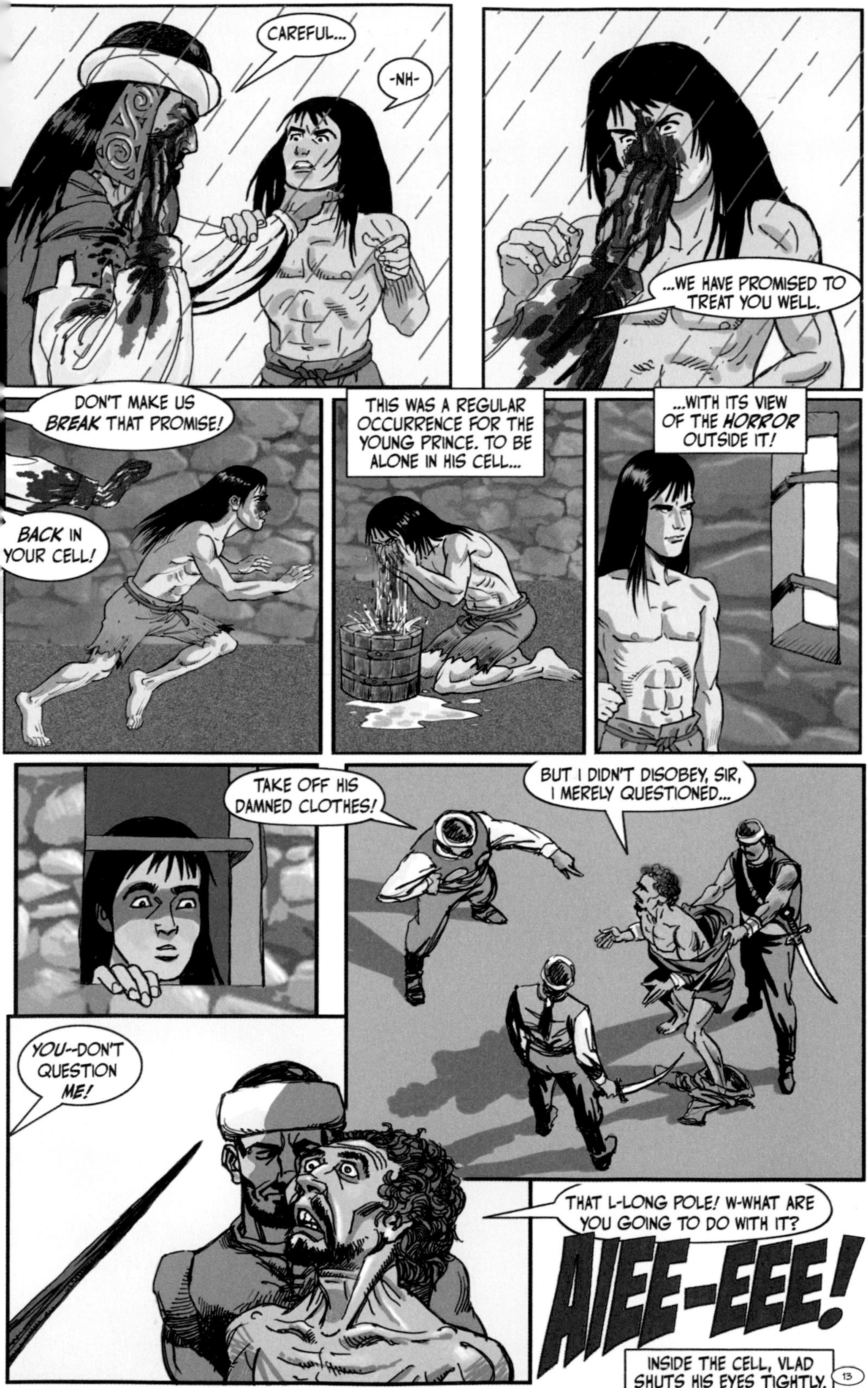
CAREFUL...
-NH-
...WE HAVE PROMISED TO TREAT YOU WELL.
DON'T MAKE US BREAK THAT PROMISE!
BACK IN YOUR CELL!
THIS WAS A REGULAR OCCURRENCE FOR THE YOUNG PRINCE. TO BE ALONE IN HIS CELL...
...WITH ITS VIEW OF THE HORROR OUTSIDE IT!
TAKE OFF HIS DAMNED CLOTHES!
BUT I DIDN'T DISOBEY, SIR, I MERELY QUESTIONED...
YOU--DON'T QUESTION ME!
THAT L-LONG POLE! W-WHAT ARE YOU GOING TO DO WITH IT?
AIEE-EEE!
INSIDE THE CELL, VLAD SHUTS HIS EYES TIGHTLY.

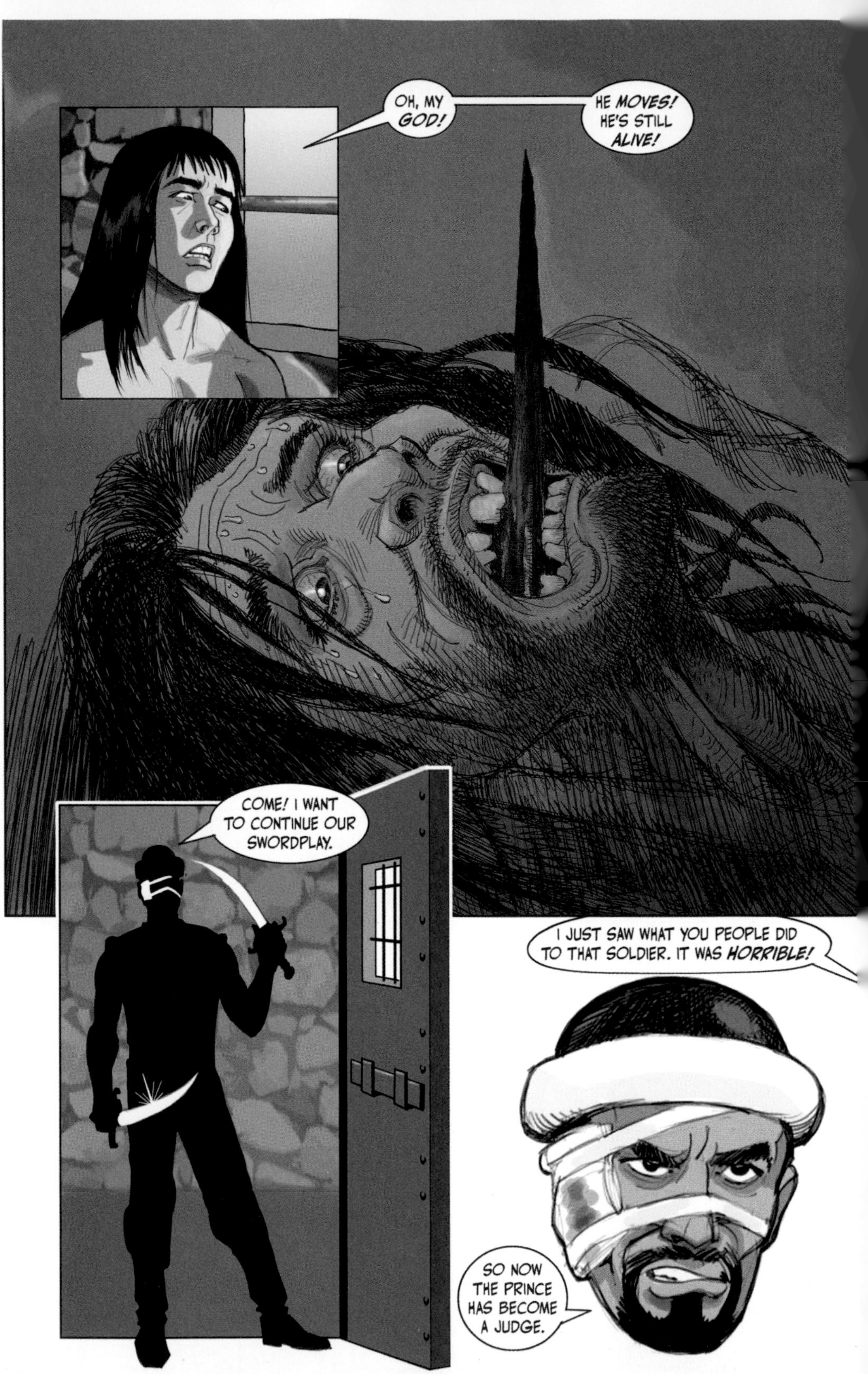
OH, MY GOD!
HE MOVES! HE'S STILL ALIVE!
COME! I WANT TO CONTINUE OUR SWORDPLAY.
I JUST SAW WHAT YOU PEOPLE DID TO THAT SOLDIER. IT WAS HORRIBLE!
SO NOW THE PRINCE HAS BECOME A JUDGE.

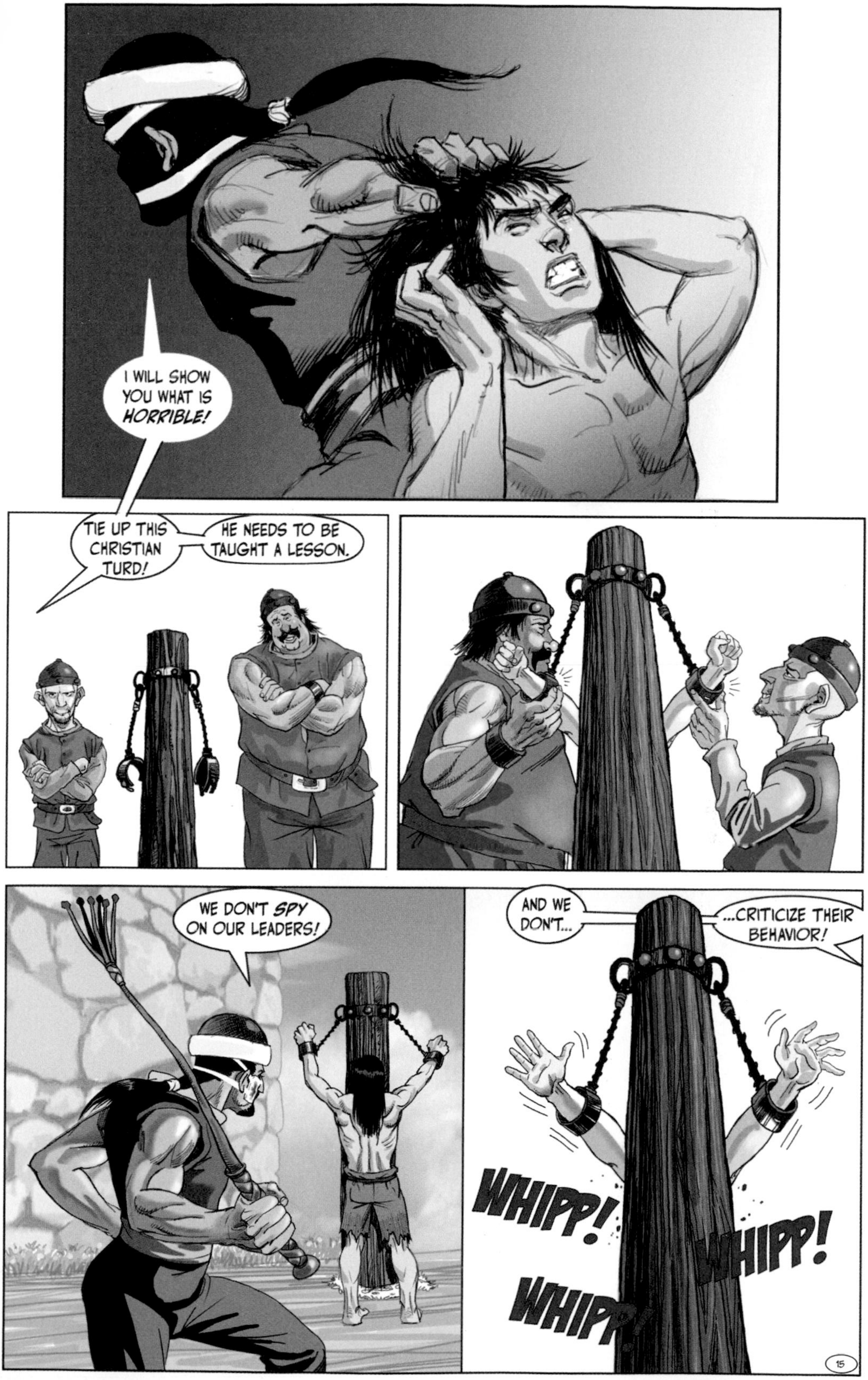
I WILL SHOW YOU WHAT IS HORRIBLE!
TIE UP THIS CHRISTIAN TURD!
HE NEEDS TO BE TAUGHT A LESSON.
WE DON'T SPY ON OUR LEADERS!
AND WE DON'T...
...CRITICIZE THEIR BEHAVIOR!
WHIPP!
WHIPP!
WHIPP!

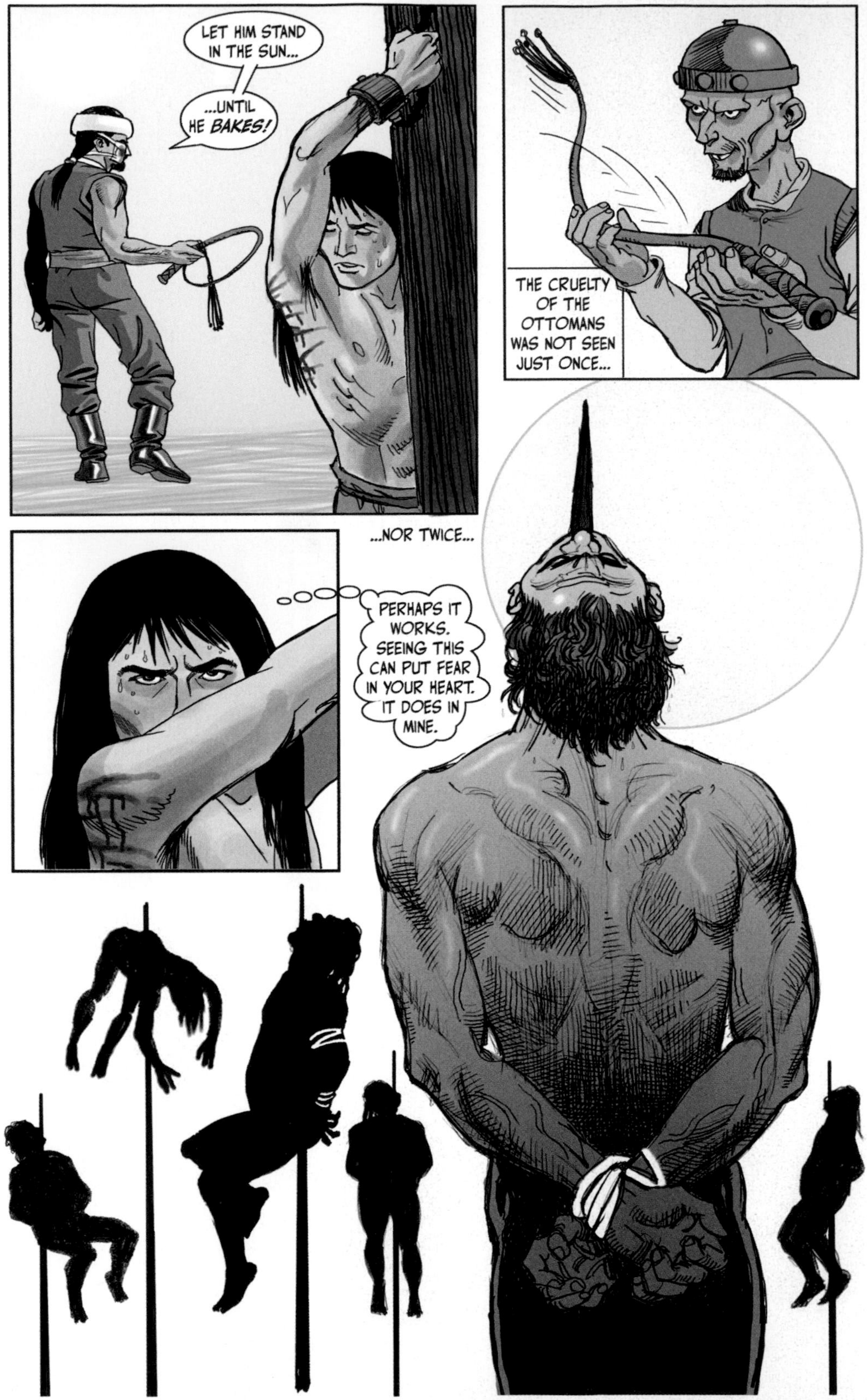
LET HIM STAND IN THE SUN...
...UNTIL HE *BAKES!*
THE CRUELTY OF THE OTTOMANS WAS NOT SEEN JUST ONCE...
...NOR TWICE...
PERHAPS IT WORKS. SEEING THIS CAN PUT FEAR IN YOUR HEART. IT DOES IN MINE.

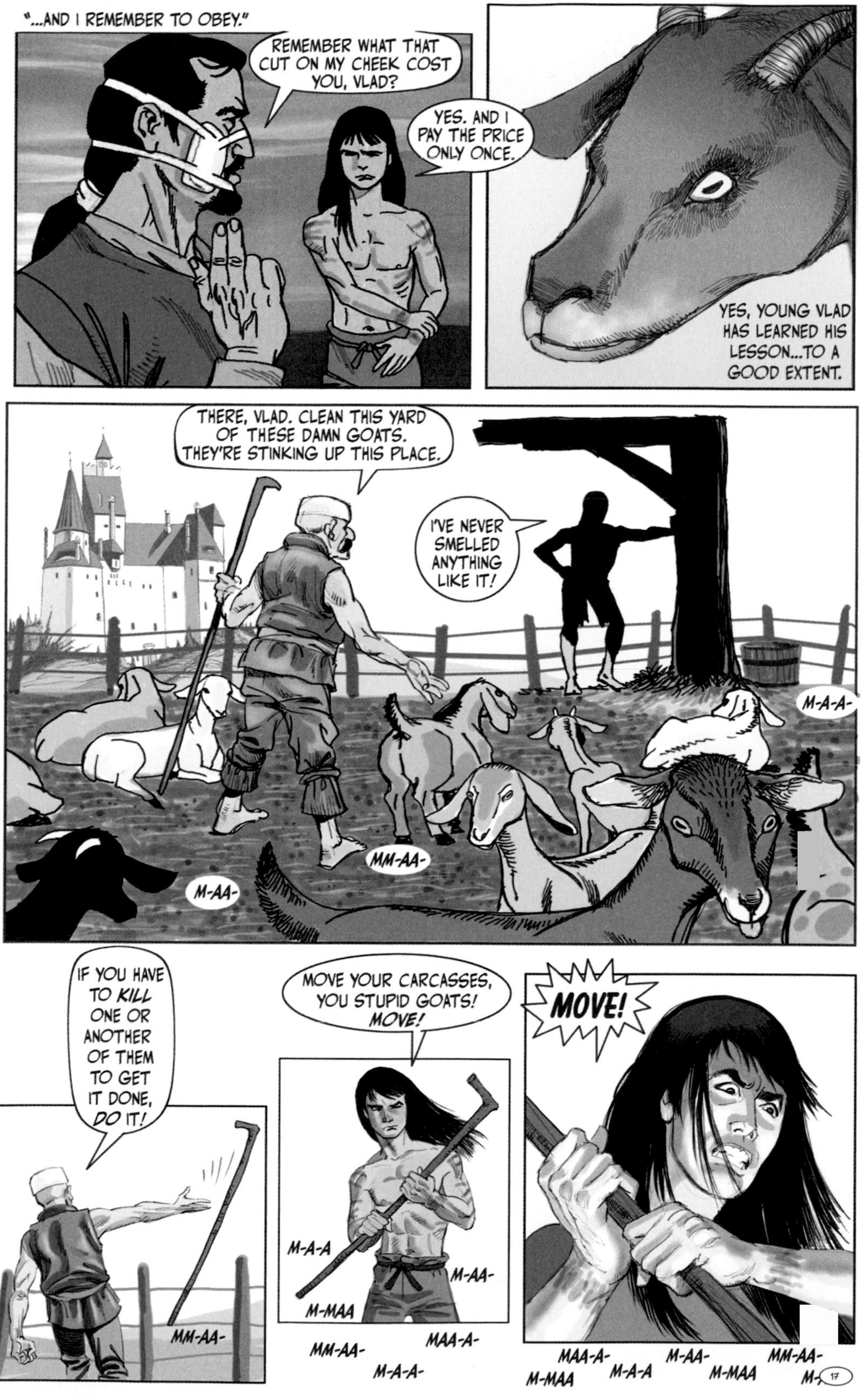
"...AND I REMEMBER TO OBEY."
REMEMBER WHAT THAT CUT ON MY CHEEK COST YOU, VLAD?
YES. AND I PAY THE PRICE ONLY ONCE.
YES, YOUNG VLAD HAS LEARNED HIS LESSON...TO A GOOD EXTENT.
THERE, VLAD. CLEAN THIS YARD OF THESE DAMN GOATS. THEY'RE STINKING UP THIS PLACE.
I'VE NEVER SMELLED ANYTHING LIKE IT!
M-A-A-
MM-AA-
M-AA-
IF YOU HAVE TO KILL ONE OR ANOTHER OF THEM TO GET IT DONE, DO IT!
MM-AA-
MOVE YOUR CARCASSES, YOU STUPID GOATS! MOVE!
M-A-A
M-AA-
M-MAA
MM-AA-
MAA-A-
M-A-A-
MOVE!
MAA-A-
M-MAA
M-A-A
M-AA-
M-MAA
MM-AA-

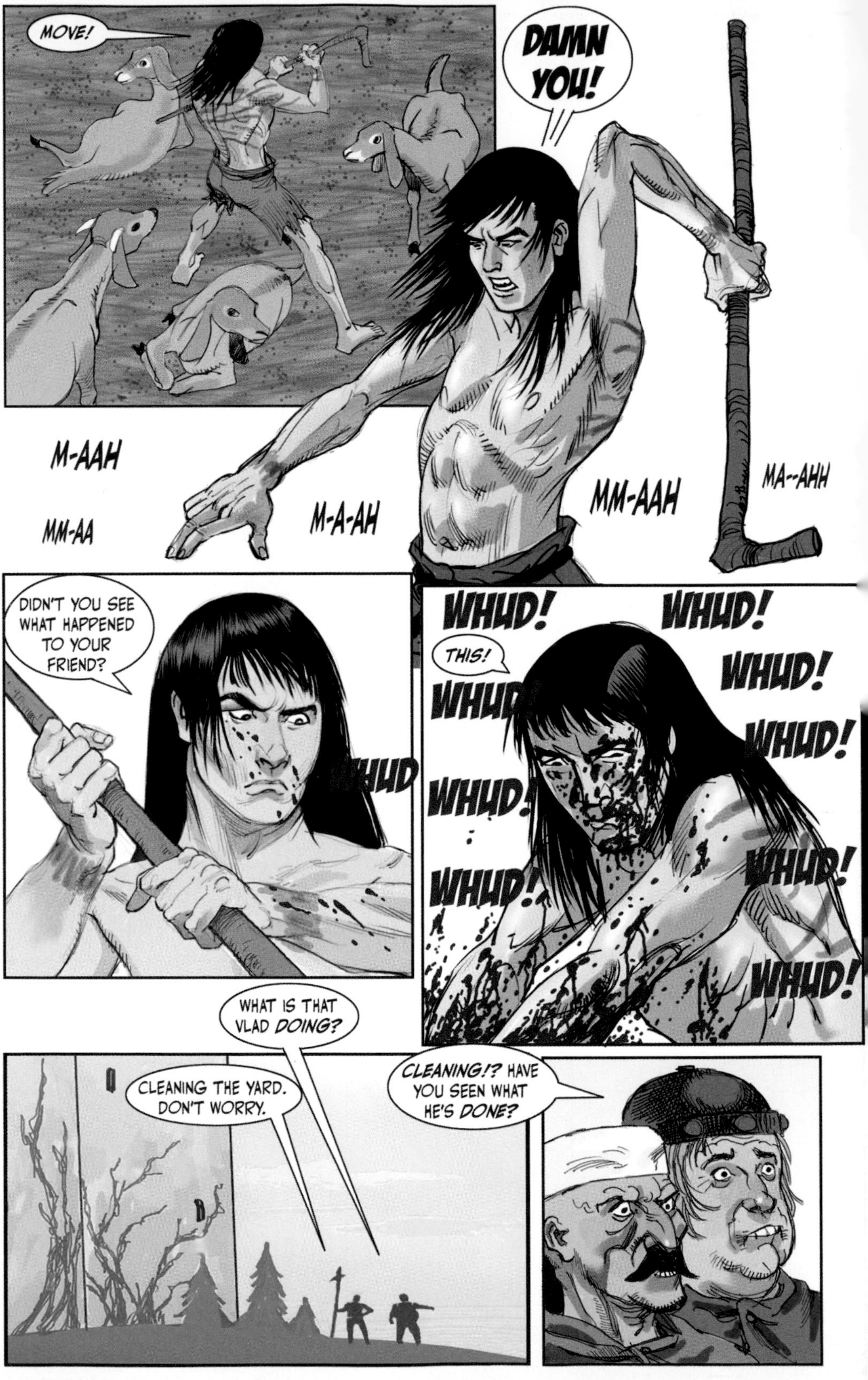

MOVE!
DAMN YOU!
M-AAH
MM-AA
M-A-AH
MM-AAH
MA--AHH
DIDN'T YOU SEE WHAT HAPPENED TO YOUR FRIEND?
WHUD
WHUD!
WHUD!
THIS!
WHUD!
WHUD!
WHUD!
WHUD!
WHUD!
WHUD!
WHUD!
WHAT IS THAT VLAD DOING?
CLEANING THE YARD. DON'T WORRY.
CLEANING!? HAVE YOU SEEN WHAT HE'S DONE?

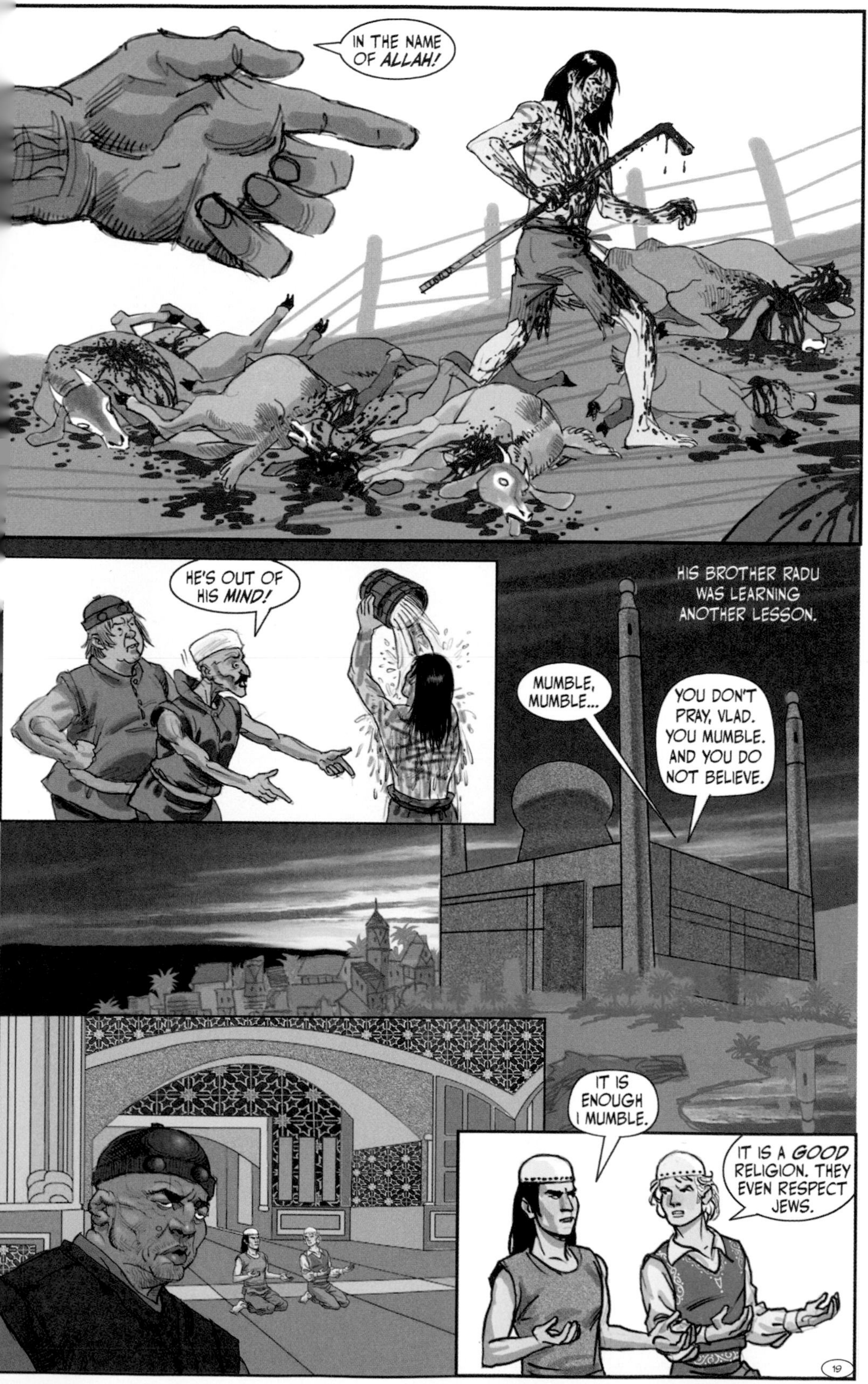
IN THE NAME OF ALLAH!
HE'S OUT OF HIS MIND!
HIS BROTHER RADU WAS LEARNING ANOTHER LESSON.
MUMBLE, MUMBLE...
YOU DON'T PRAY, VLAD. YOU MUMBLE. AND YOU DO NOT BELIEVE.
IT IS ENOUGH I MUMBLE.
IT IS A GOOD RELIGION. THEY EVEN RESPECT JEWS.

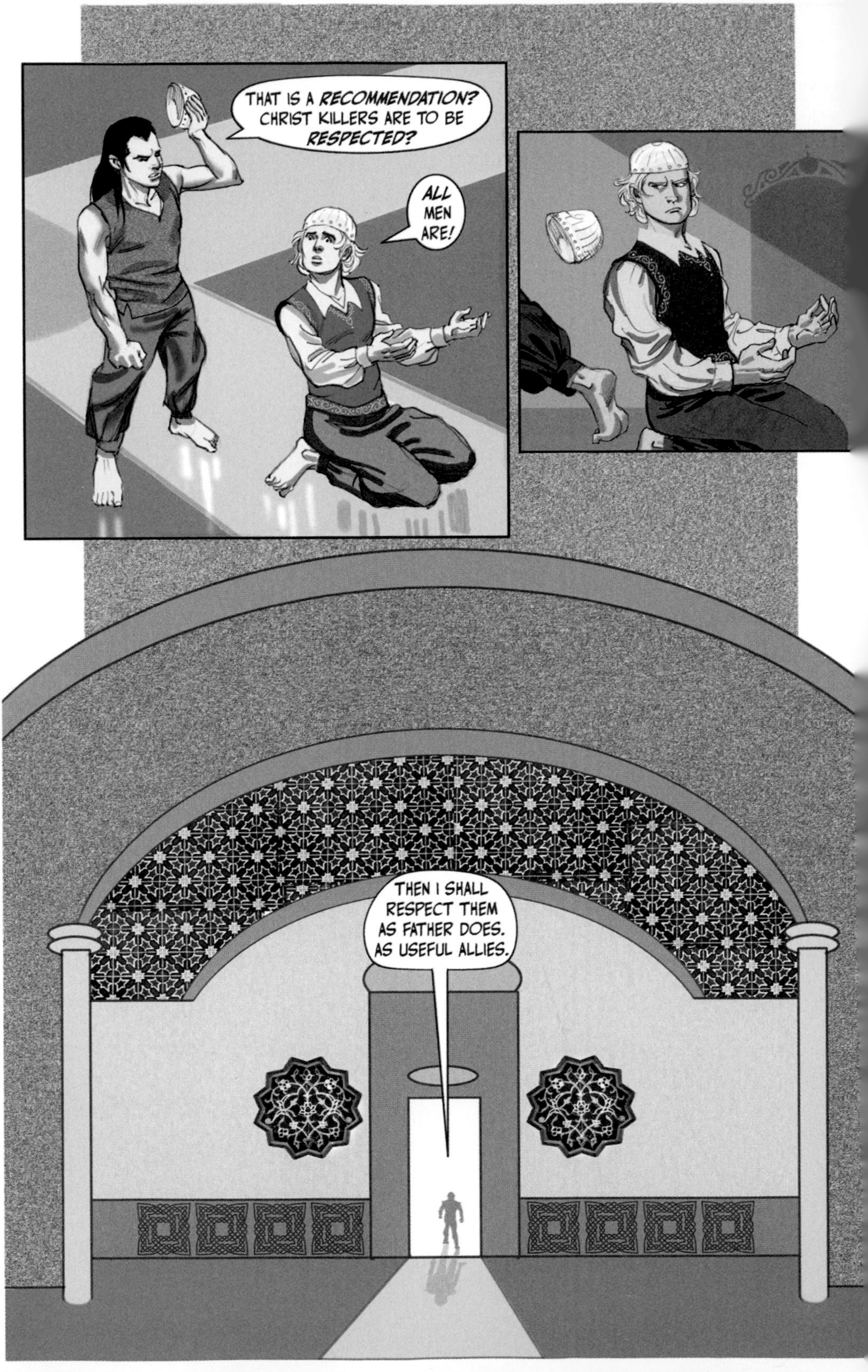
THAT IS A *RECOMMENDATION?* CHRIST KILLERS ARE TO BE *RESPECTED?*
ALL MEN ARE!
THEN I SHALL RESPECT THEM AS FATHER DOES. AS USEFUL ALLIES.

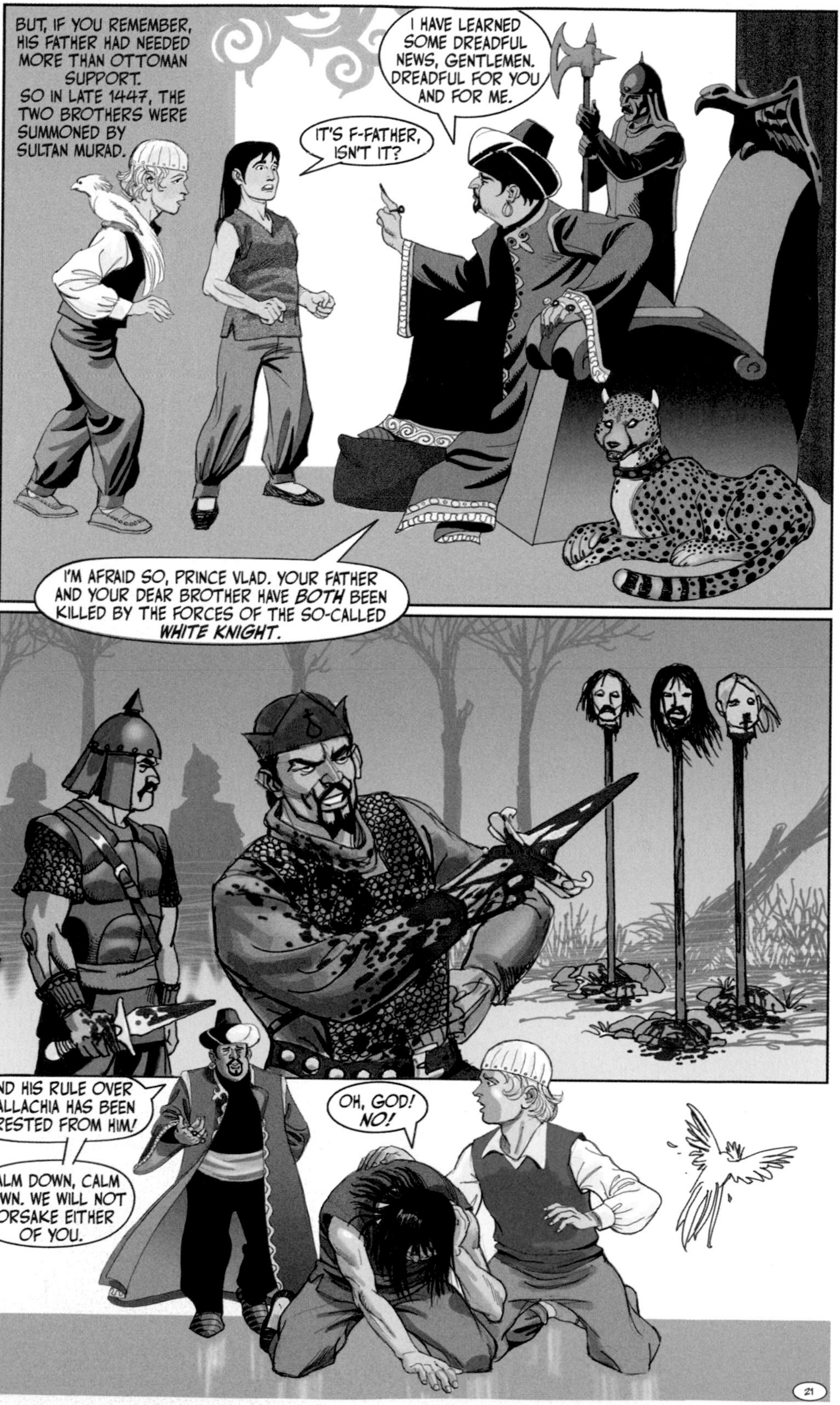
BUT, IF YOU REMEMBER, HIS FATHER HAD NEEDED MORE THAN OTTOMAN SUPPORT. SO IN LATE 1447, THE TWO BROTHERS WERE SUMMONED BY SULTAN MURAD.
I HAVE LEARNED SOME DREADFUL NEWS, GENTLEMEN. DREADFUL FOR YOU AND FOR ME.
IT'S F-FATHER, ISN'T IT?
I'M AFRAID SO, PRINCE VLAD. YOUR FATHER AND YOUR DEAR BROTHER HAVE *BOTH* BEEN KILLED BY THE FORCES OF THE SO-CALLED *WHITE KNIGHT*.
AND HIS RULE OVER WALLACHIA HAS BEEN WRESTED FROM HIM!
CALM DOWN, CALM DOWN. WE WILL NOT FORSAKE EITHER OF YOU.
OH, GOD! *NO!*

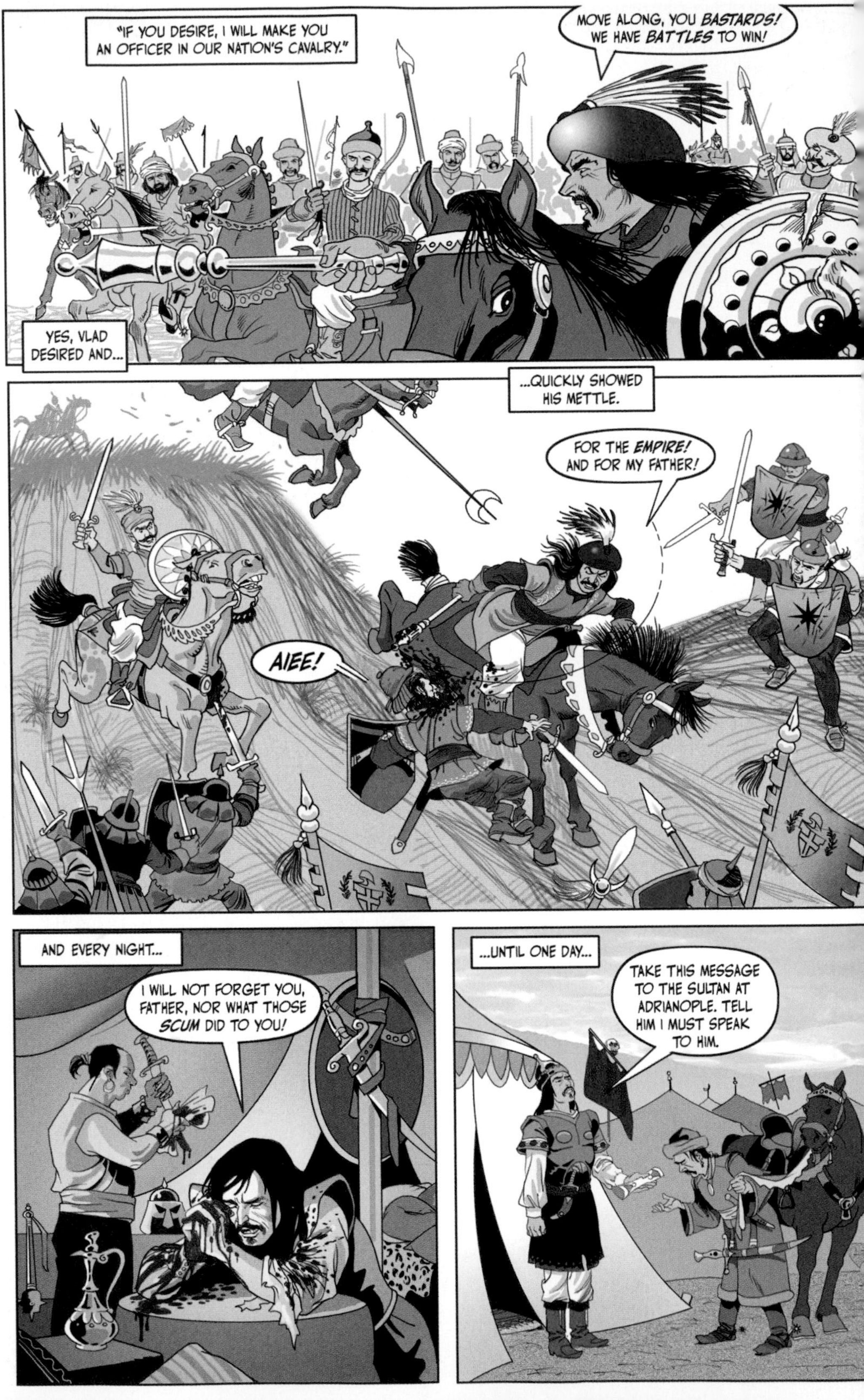
"IF YOU DESIRE, I WILL MAKE YOU AN OFFICER IN OUR NATION'S CAVALRY."
MOVE ALONG, YOU BASTARDS! WE HAVE BATTLES TO WIN!
YES, VLAD DESIRED AND...
...QUICKLY SHOWED HIS METTLE.
FOR THE EMPIRE! AND FOR MY FATHER!
AIEE!
AND EVERY NIGHT...
I WILL NOT FORGET YOU, FATHER, NOR WHAT THOSE SCUM DID TO YOU!
...UNTIL ONE DAY...
TAKE THIS MESSAGE TO THE SULTAN AT ADRIANOPLE. TELL HIM I MUST SPEAK TO HIM.

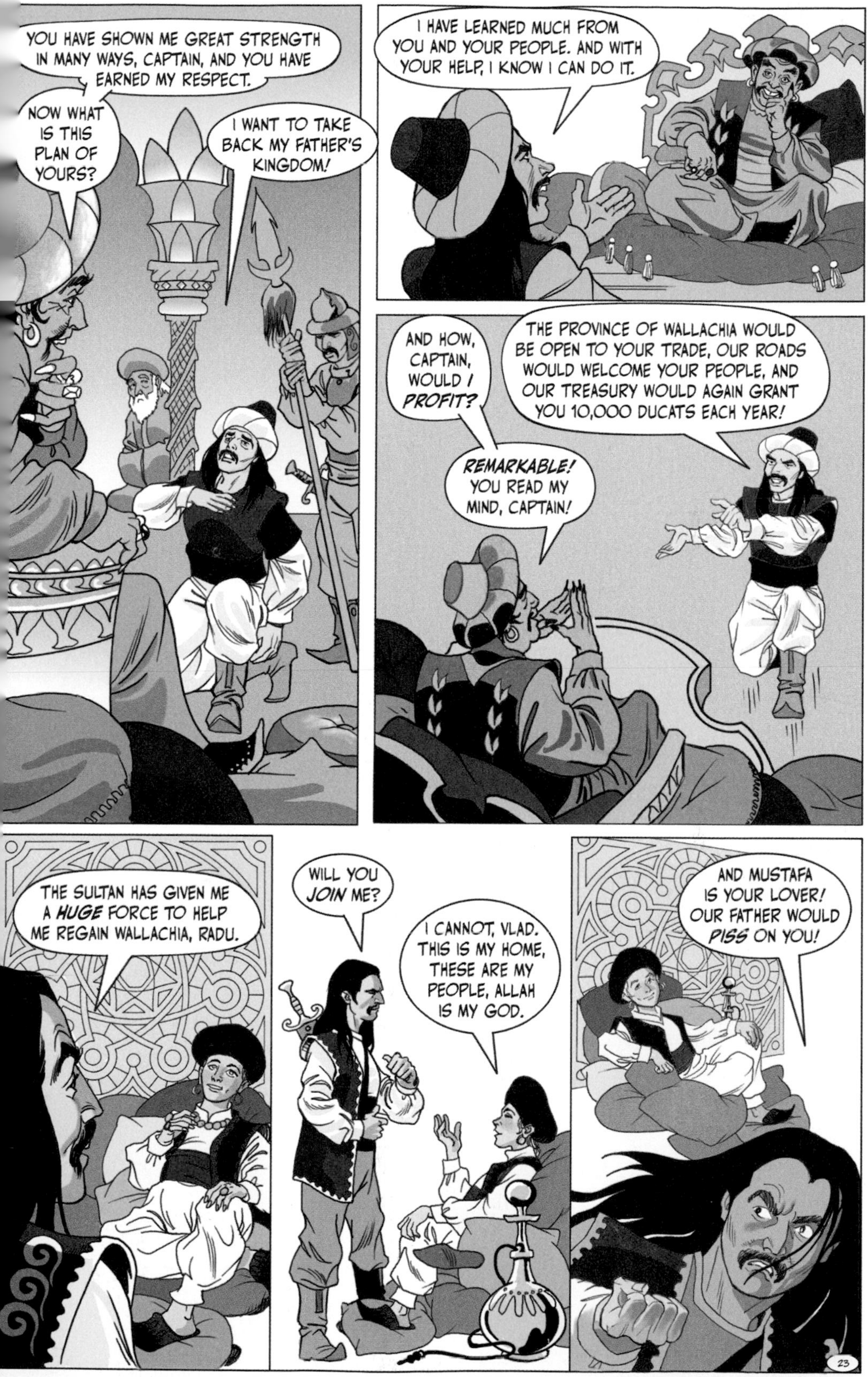
YOU HAVE SHOWN ME GREAT STRENGTH IN MANY WAYS, CAPTAIN, AND YOU HAVE EARNED MY RESPECT.
NOW WHAT IS THIS PLAN OF YOURS?
I WANT TO TAKE BACK MY FATHER'S KINGDOM!
I HAVE LEARNED MUCH FROM YOU AND YOUR PEOPLE. AND WITH YOUR HELP, I KNOW I CAN DO IT.
AND HOW, CAPTAIN, WOULD *I* *PROFIT?*
THE PROVINCE OF WALLACHIA WOULD BE OPEN TO YOUR TRADE, OUR ROADS WOULD WELCOME YOUR PEOPLE, AND OUR TREASURY WOULD AGAIN GRANT YOU 10,000 DUCATS EACH YEAR!
REMARKABLE! YOU READ MY MIND, CAPTAIN!
THE SULTAN HAS GIVEN ME A *HUGE* FORCE TO HELP ME REGAIN WALLACHIA, RADU.
WILL YOU *JOIN* ME?
I CANNOT, VLAD. THIS IS MY HOME, THESE ARE MY PEOPLE, ALLAH IS MY GOD.
AND MUSTAFA IS YOUR LOVER! OUR FATHER WOULD *PISS* ON YOU!

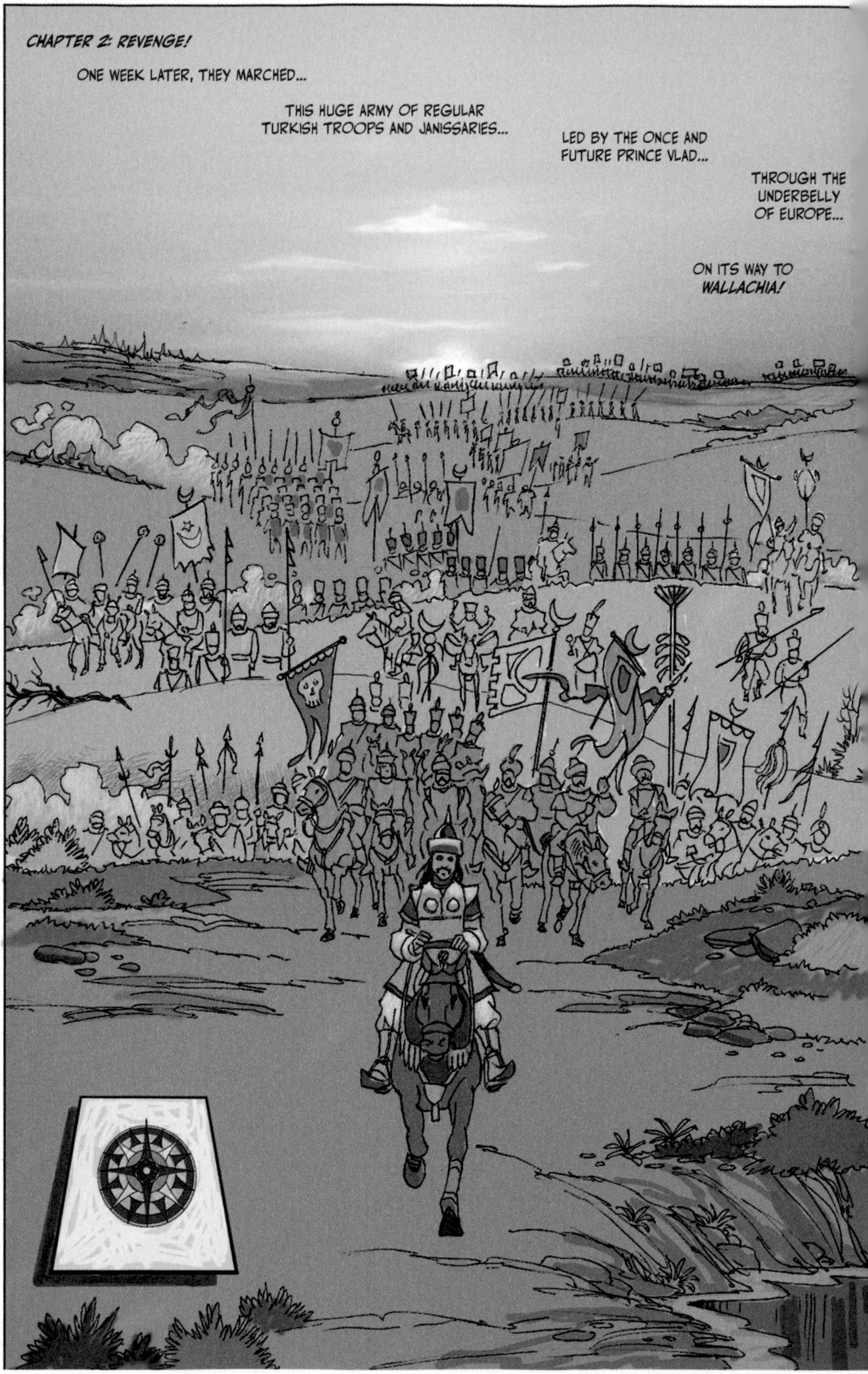
CHAPTER 2: REVENGE!
ONE WEEK LATER, THEY MARCHED...
THIS HUGE ARMY OF REGULAR TURKISH TROOPS AND JANISSARIES...
LED BY THE ONCE AND FUTURE PRINCE VLAD...
THROUGH THE UNDERBELLY OF EUROPE...
ON ITS WAY TO WALLACHIA!

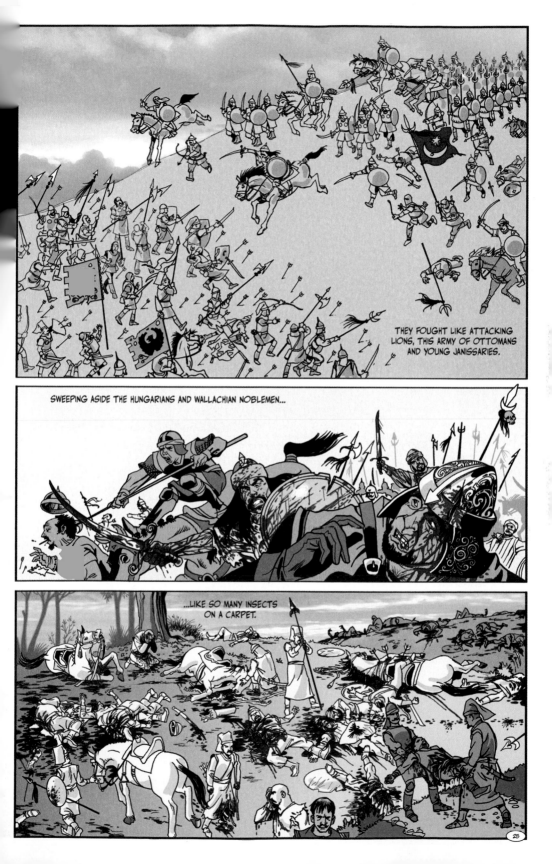

THEY FOUGHT LIKE ATTACKING LIONS, THIS ARMY OF OTTOMANS AND YOUNG JANISSARIES.

SWEEPING ASIDE THE HUNGARIANS AND WALLACHIAN NOBLEMEN...

...LIKE SO MANY INSECTS ON A CARPET.

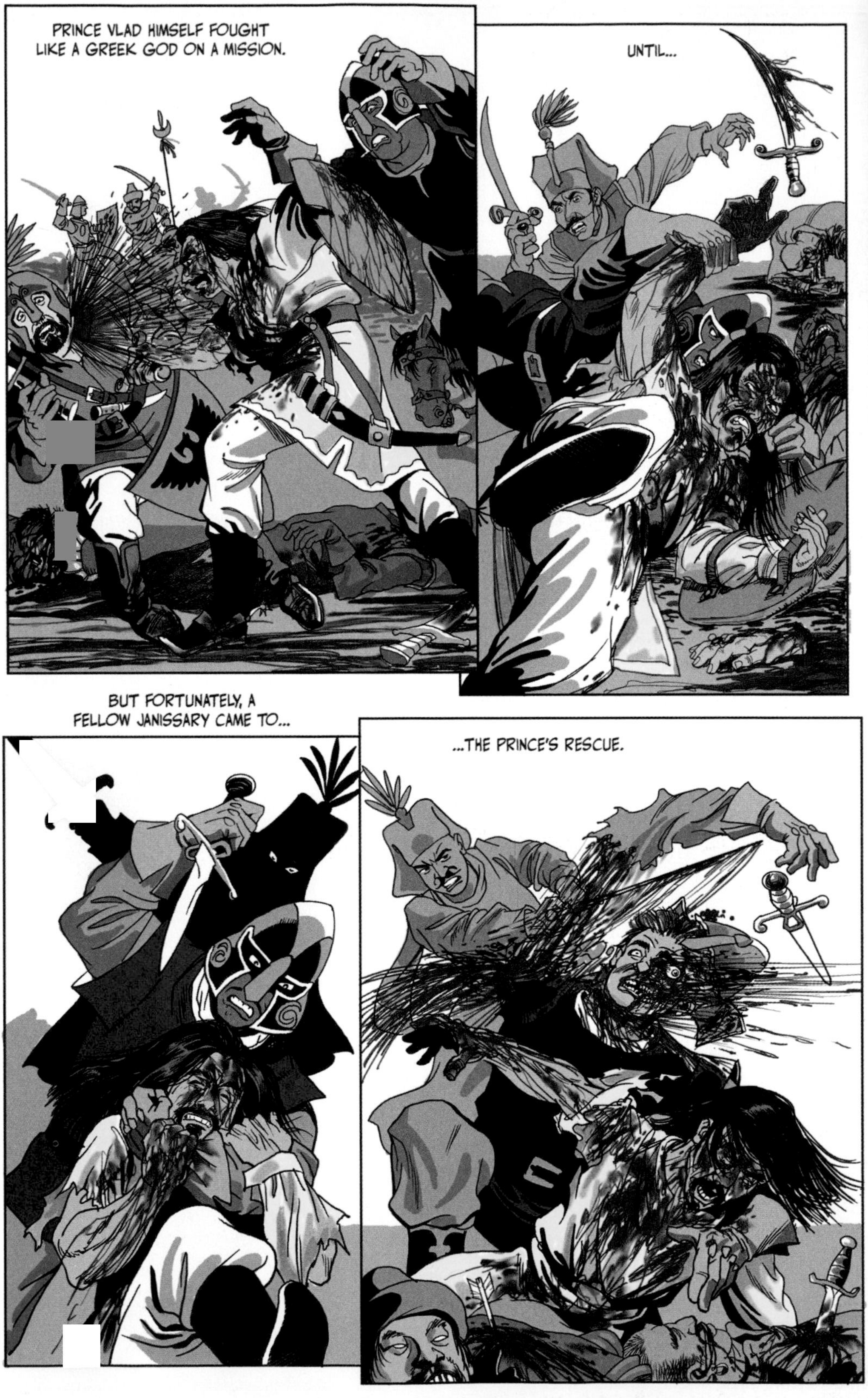
PRINCE VLAD HIMSELF FOUGHT LIKE A GREEK GOD ON A MISSION.
UNTIL...
BUT FORTUNATELY, A FELLOW JANISSARY CAME TO...
...THE PRINCE'S RESCUE.

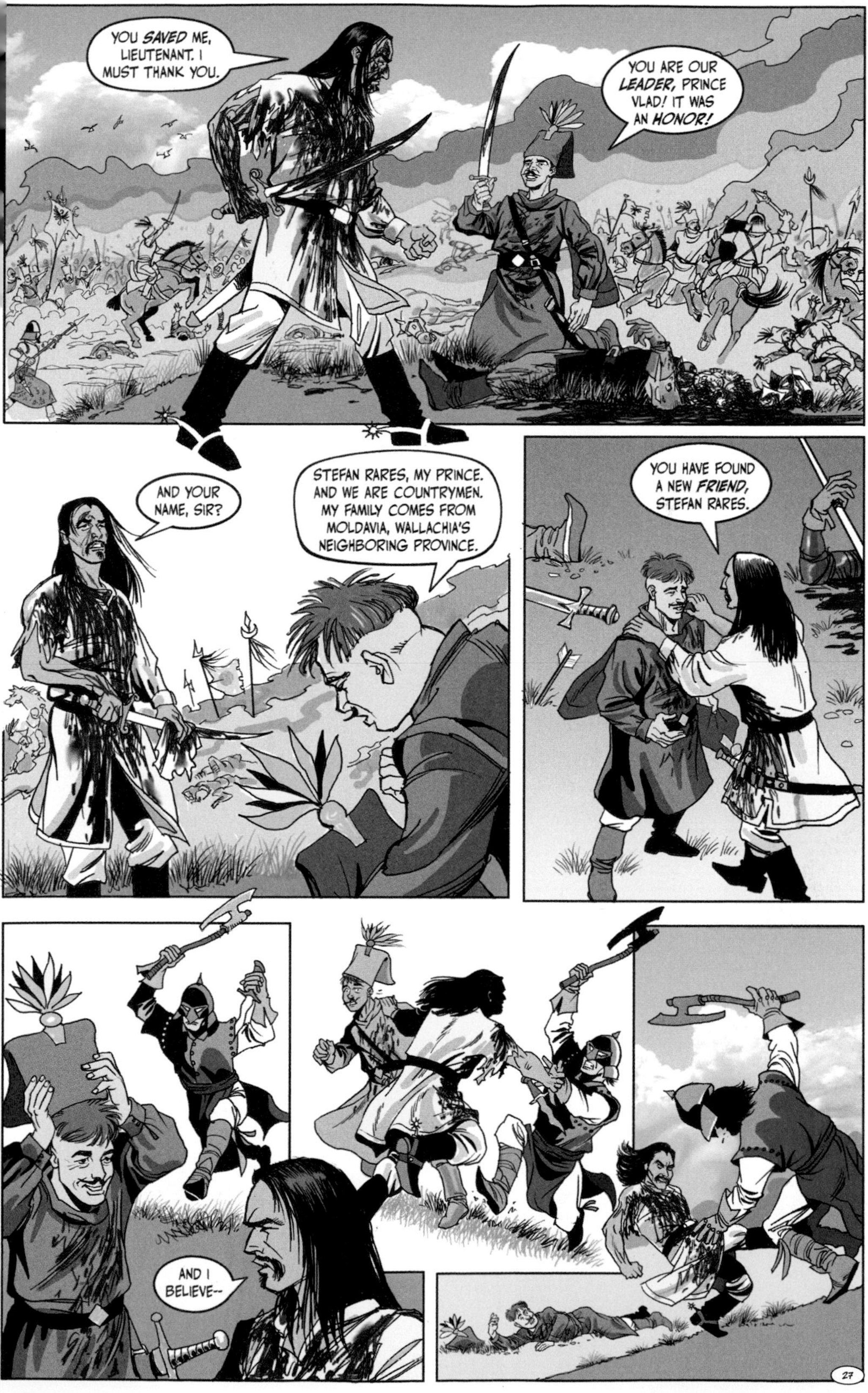

YOU SAVED ME, LIEUTENANT. I MUST THANK YOU.
YOU ARE OUR LEADER, PRINCE VLAD! IT WAS AN HONOR!
AND YOUR NAME, SIR?
STEFAN RARES, MY PRINCE. AND WE ARE COUNTRYMEN. MY FAMILY COMES FROM MOLDAVIA, WALLACHIA'S NEIGHBORING PROVINCE.
YOU HAVE FOUND A NEW FRIEND, STEFAN RARES.
AND I BELIEVE--

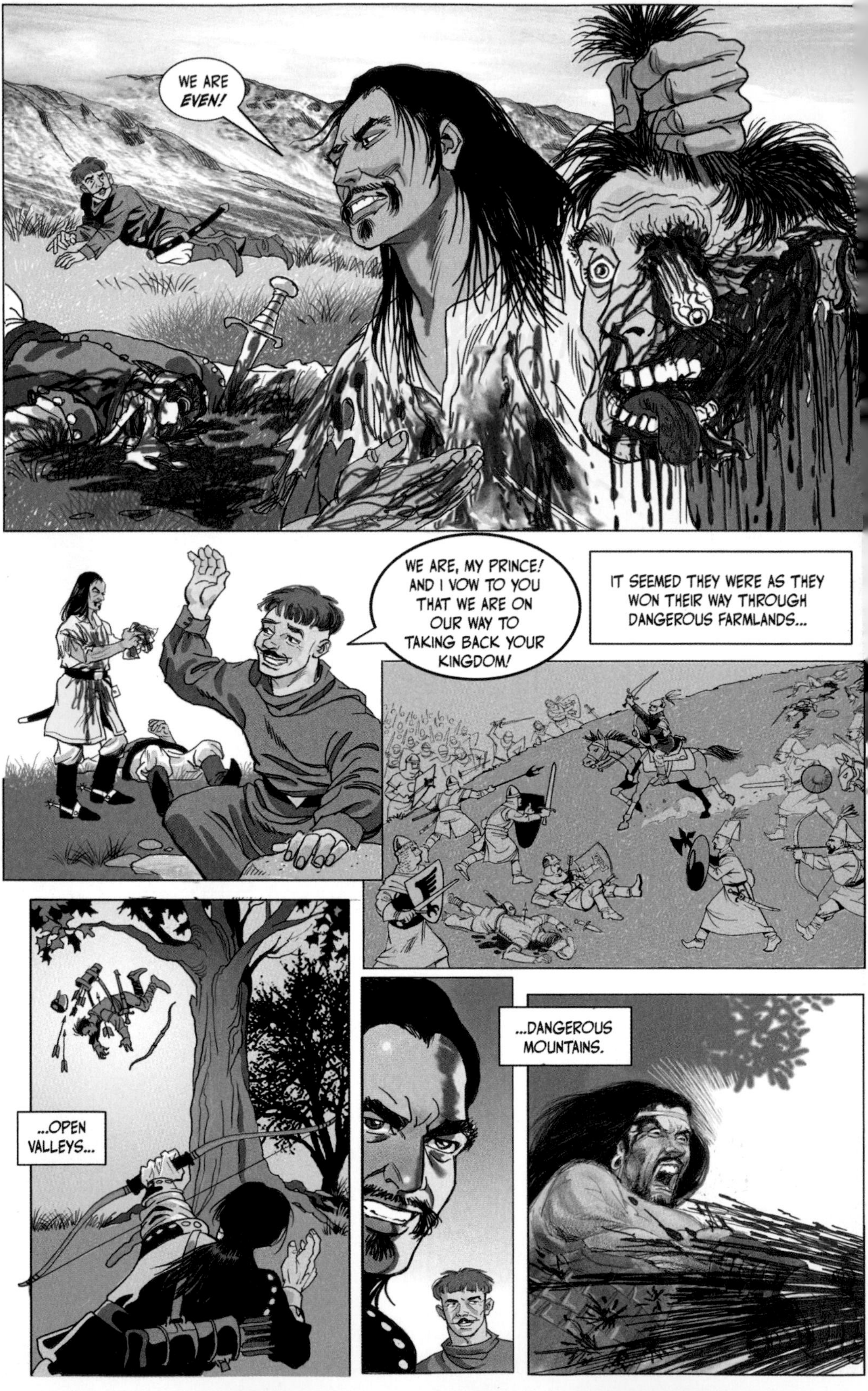
WE ARE *EVEN!*
WE ARE, MY PRINCE! AND I VOW TO YOU THAT WE ARE ON OUR WAY TO TAKING BACK YOUR KINGDOM!
IT SEEMED THEY WERE AS THEY WON THEIR WAY THROUGH DANGEROUS FARMLANDS...
...OPEN VALLEYS...
...DANGEROUS MOUNTAINS.

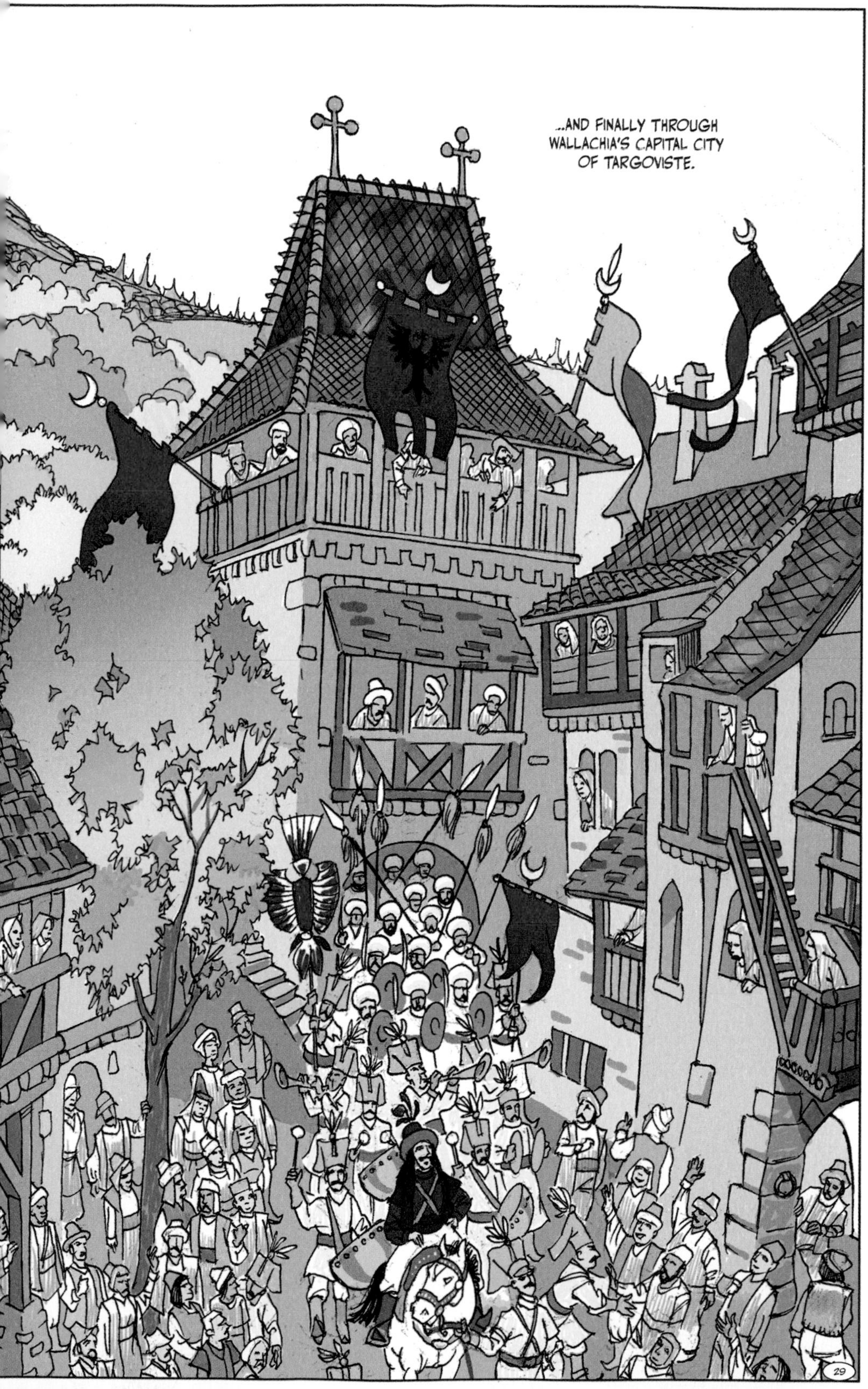
...AND FINALLY THROUGH WALLACHIA'S CAPITAL CITY OF TARGOVISTE.

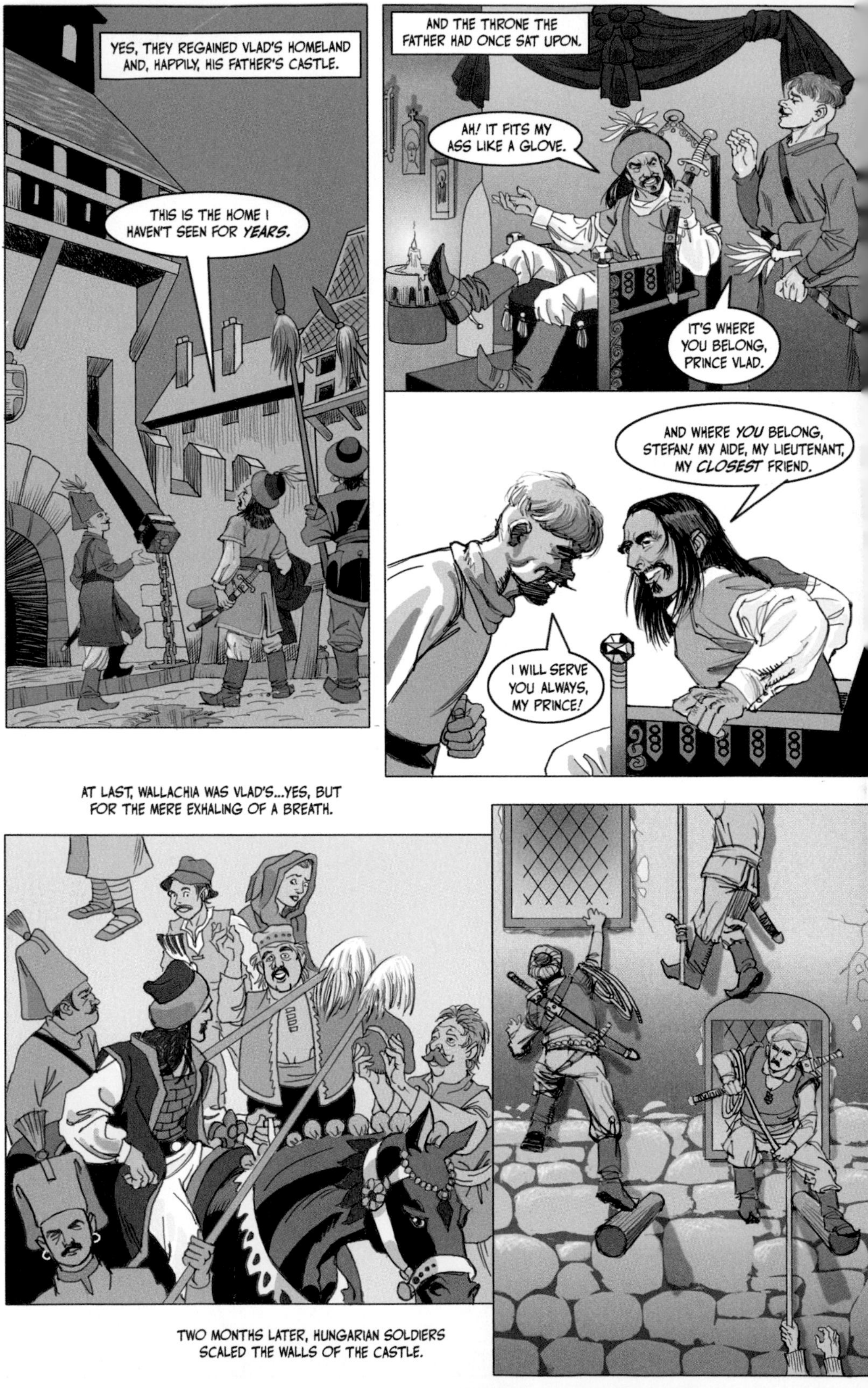
YES, THEY REGAINED VLAD'S HOMELAND AND, HAPPILY, HIS FATHER'S CASTLE.
THIS IS THE HOME I HAVEN'T SEEN FOR *YEARS.*
AND THE THRONE THE FATHER HAD ONCE SAT UPON.
AH! IT FITS MY ASS LIKE A GLOVE.
IT'S WHERE YOU BELONG, PRINCE VLAD.
AND WHERE *YOU* BELONG, STEFAN! MY AIDE, MY LIEUTENANT, MY *CLOSEST* FRIEND.
I WILL SERVE YOU ALWAYS, MY PRINCE!
AT LAST, WALLACHIA WAS VLAD'S...YES, BUT FOR THE MERE EXHALING OF A BREATH.
TWO MONTHS LATER, HUNGARIAN SOLDIERS SCALED THE WALLS OF THE CASTLE.

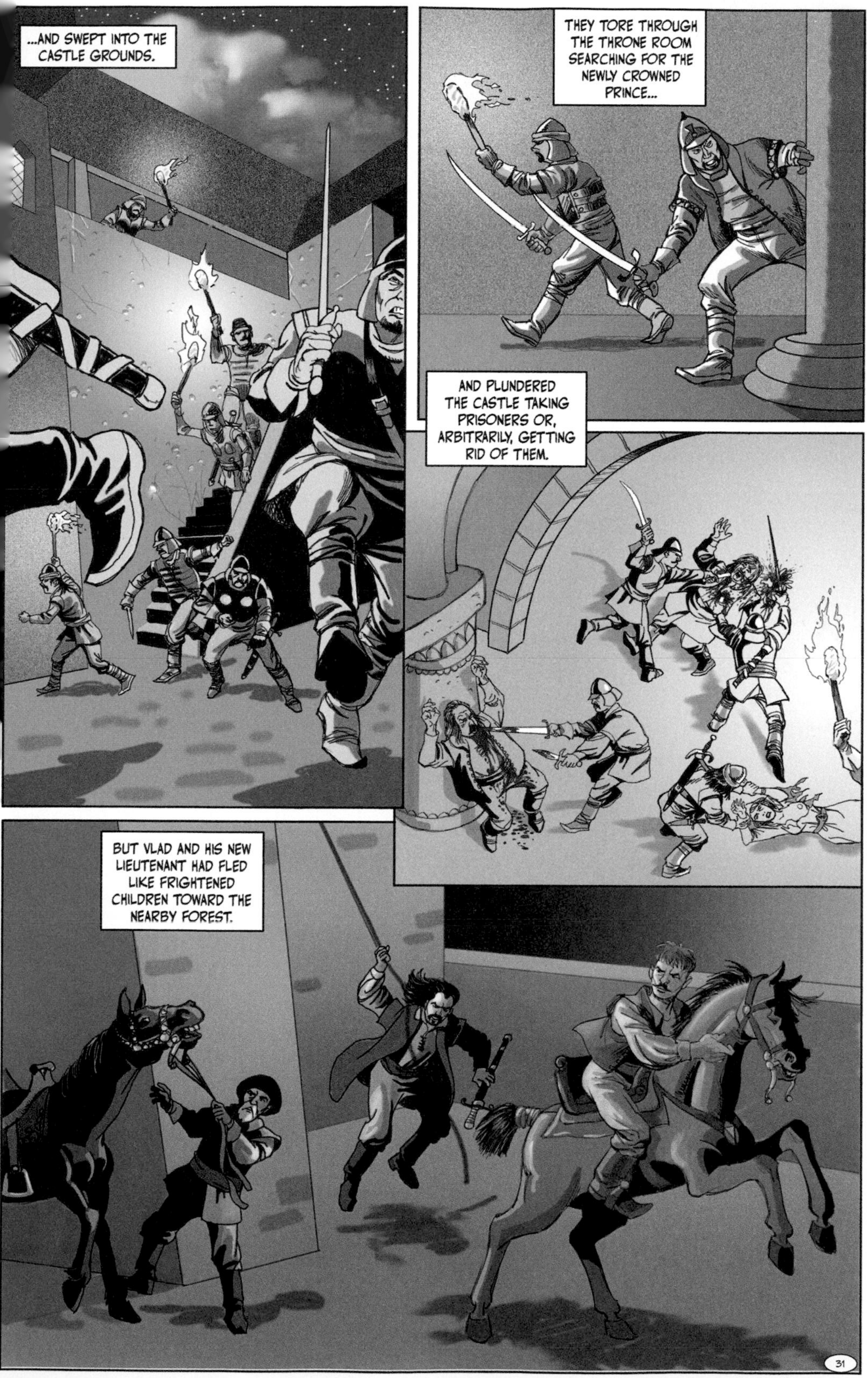
...AND SWEPT INTO THE CASTLE GROUNDS.
THEY TORE THROUGH THE THRONE ROOM SEARCHING FOR THE NEWLY CROWNED PRINCE...
AND PLUNDERED THE CASTLE TAKING PRISONERS OR, ARBITRARILY, GETTING RID OF THEM.
BUT VLAD AND HIS NEW LIEUTENANT HAD FLED LIKE FRIGHTENED CHILDREN TOWARD THE NEARBY FOREST.

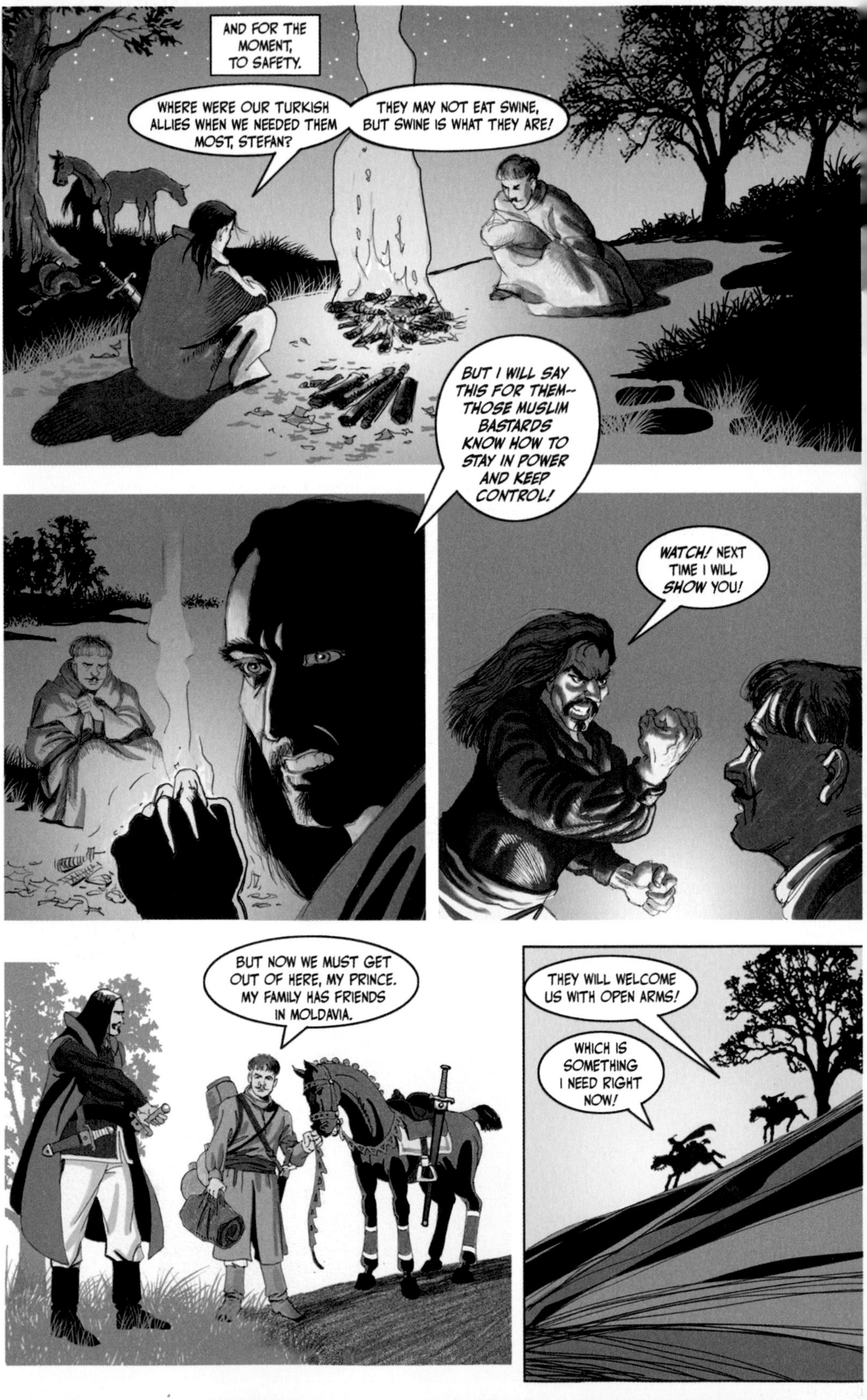
AND FOR THE MOMENT, TO SAFETY.
WHERE WERE OUR TURKISH ALLIES WHEN WE NEEDED THEM MOST, STEFAN?
THEY MAY NOT EAT SWINE, BUT SWINE IS WHAT THEY ARE!
BUT I WILL SAY THIS FOR THEM-- THOSE MUSLIM BASTARDS KNOW HOW TO STAY IN POWER AND KEEP CONTROL!
WATCH! NEXT TIME I WILL SHOW YOU!
BUT NOW WE MUST GET OUT OF HERE, MY PRINCE. MY FAMILY HAS FRIENDS IN MOLDAVIA.
THEY WILL WELCOME US WITH OPEN ARMS!
WHICH IS SOMETHING I NEED RIGHT NOW!

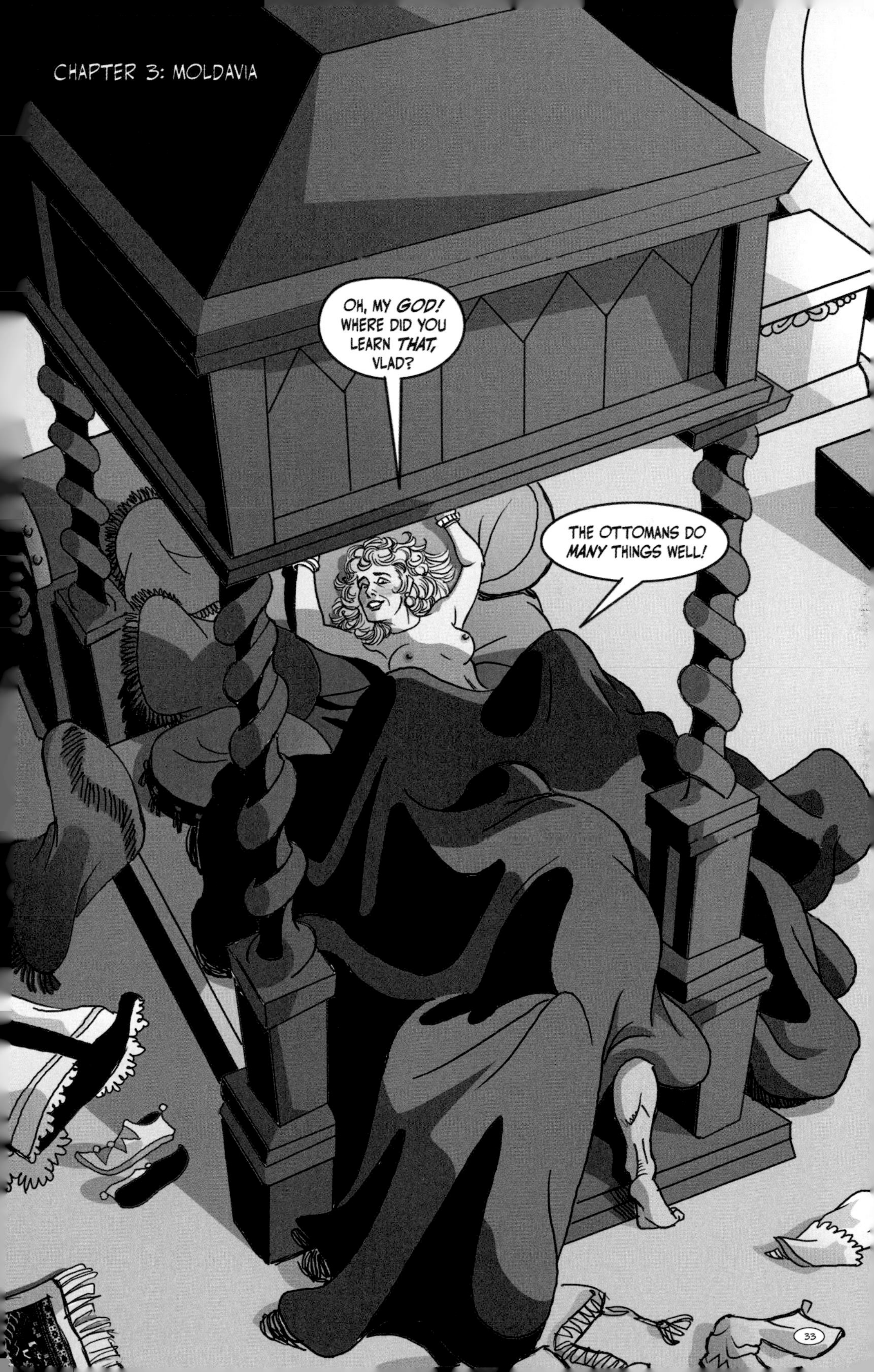
CHAPTER 3: MOLDAVIA
OH, MY *GOD!* WHERE DID YOU LEARN *THAT,* VLAD?
THE OTTOMANS DO *MANY* THINGS WELL!

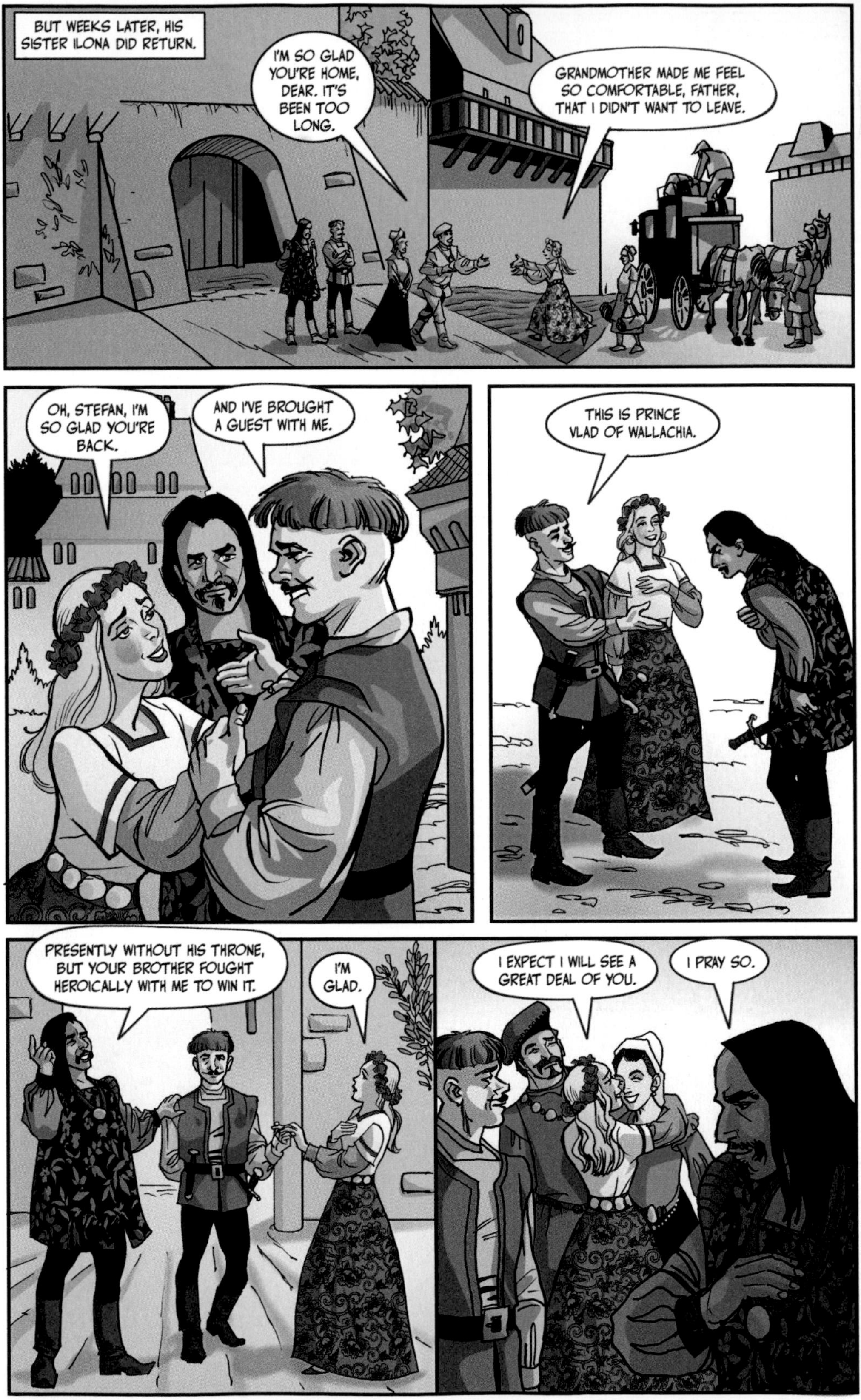
BUT WEEKS LATER, HIS SISTER ILONA DID RETURN.
I'M SO GLAD YOU'RE HOME, DEAR. IT'S BEEN TOO LONG.
GRANDMOTHER MADE ME FEEL SO COMFORTABLE, FATHER, THAT I DIDN'T WANT TO LEAVE.
OH, STEFAN, I'M SO GLAD YOU'RE BACK.
AND I'VE BROUGHT A GUEST WITH ME.
THIS IS PRINCE VLAD OF WALLACHIA.
PRESENTLY WITHOUT HIS THRONE, BUT YOUR BROTHER FOUGHT HEROICALLY WITH ME TO WIN IT.
I'M GLAD.
I EXPECT I WILL SEE A GREAT DEAL OF YOU.
I PRAY SO.

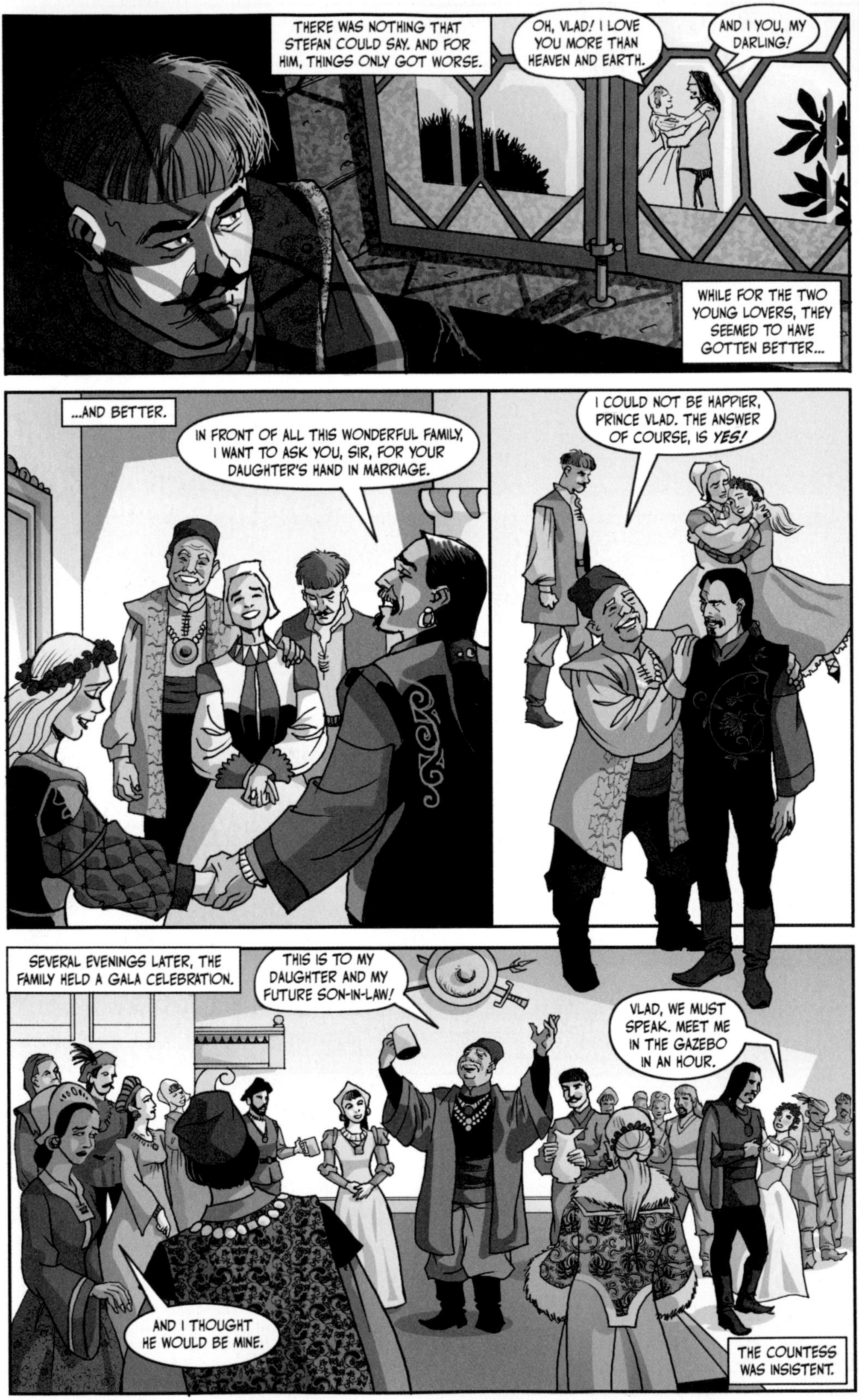

THERE WAS NOTHING THAT STEFAN COULD SAY. AND FOR HIM, THINGS ONLY GOT WORSE.
OH, VLAD! I LOVE YOU MORE THAN HEAVEN AND EARTH.
AND I YOU, MY DARLING!
WHILE FOR THE TWO YOUNG LOVERS, THEY SEEMED TO HAVE GOTTEN BETTER...
...AND BETTER.
IN FRONT OF ALL THIS WONDERFUL FAMILY, I WANT TO ASK YOU, SIR, FOR YOUR DAUGHTER'S HAND IN MARRIAGE.
I COULD NOT BE HAPPIER, PRINCE VLAD. THE ANSWER OF COURSE, IS YES!
SEVERAL EVENINGS LATER, THE FAMILY HELD A GALA CELEBRATION.
THIS IS TO MY DAUGHTER AND MY FUTURE SON-IN-LAW!
VLAD, WE MUST SPEAK. MEET ME IN THE GAZEBO IN AN HOUR.
AND I THOUGHT HE WOULD BE MINE.
THE COUNTESS WAS INSISTENT.

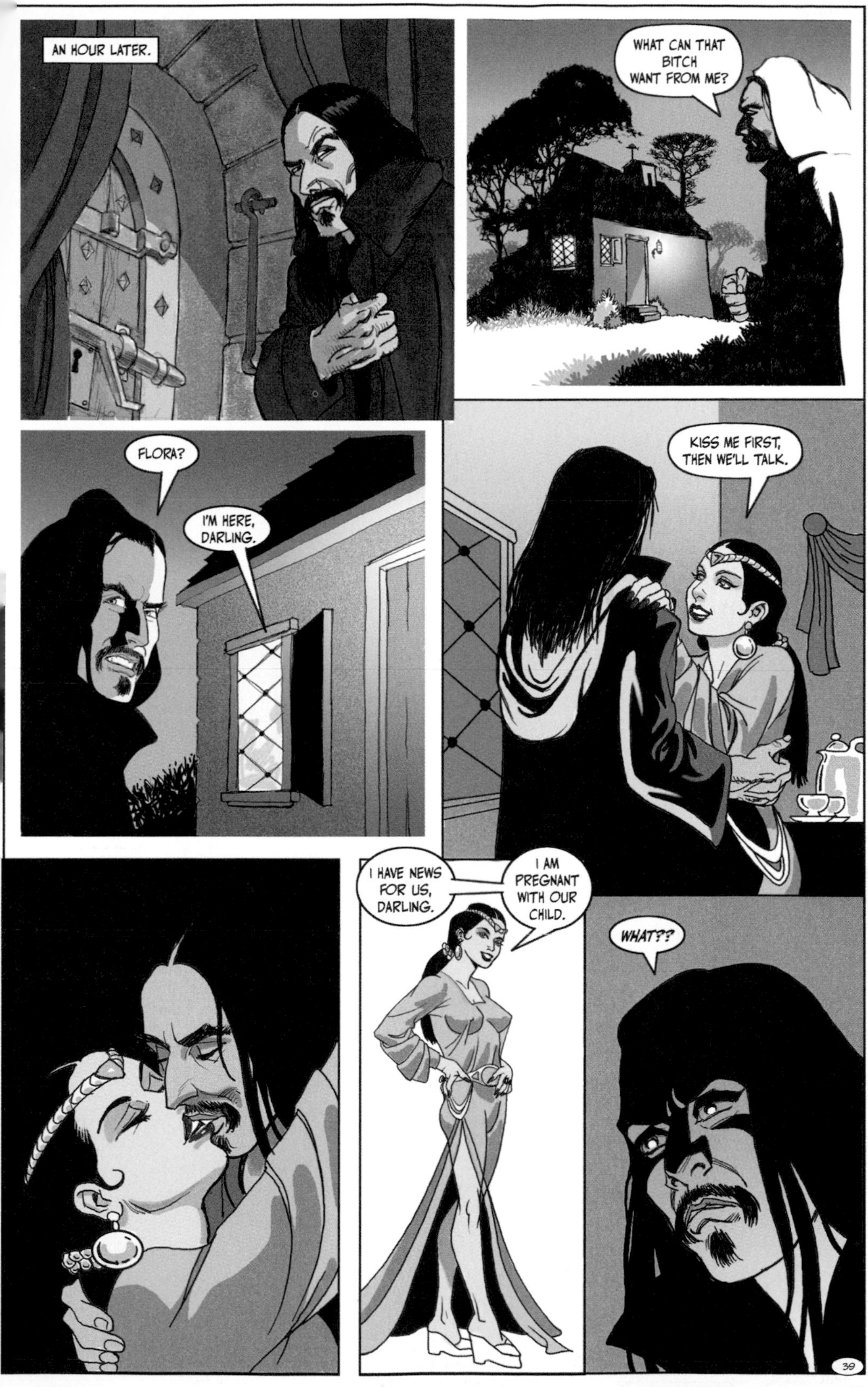
AN HOUR LATER.
WHAT CAN THAT BITCH WANT FROM ME?
FLORA?
I'M HERE, DARLING.
KISS ME FIRST, THEN WE'LL TALK.
I HAVE NEWS FOR US, DARLING.
I AM PREGNANT WITH OUR CHILD.
WHAT??

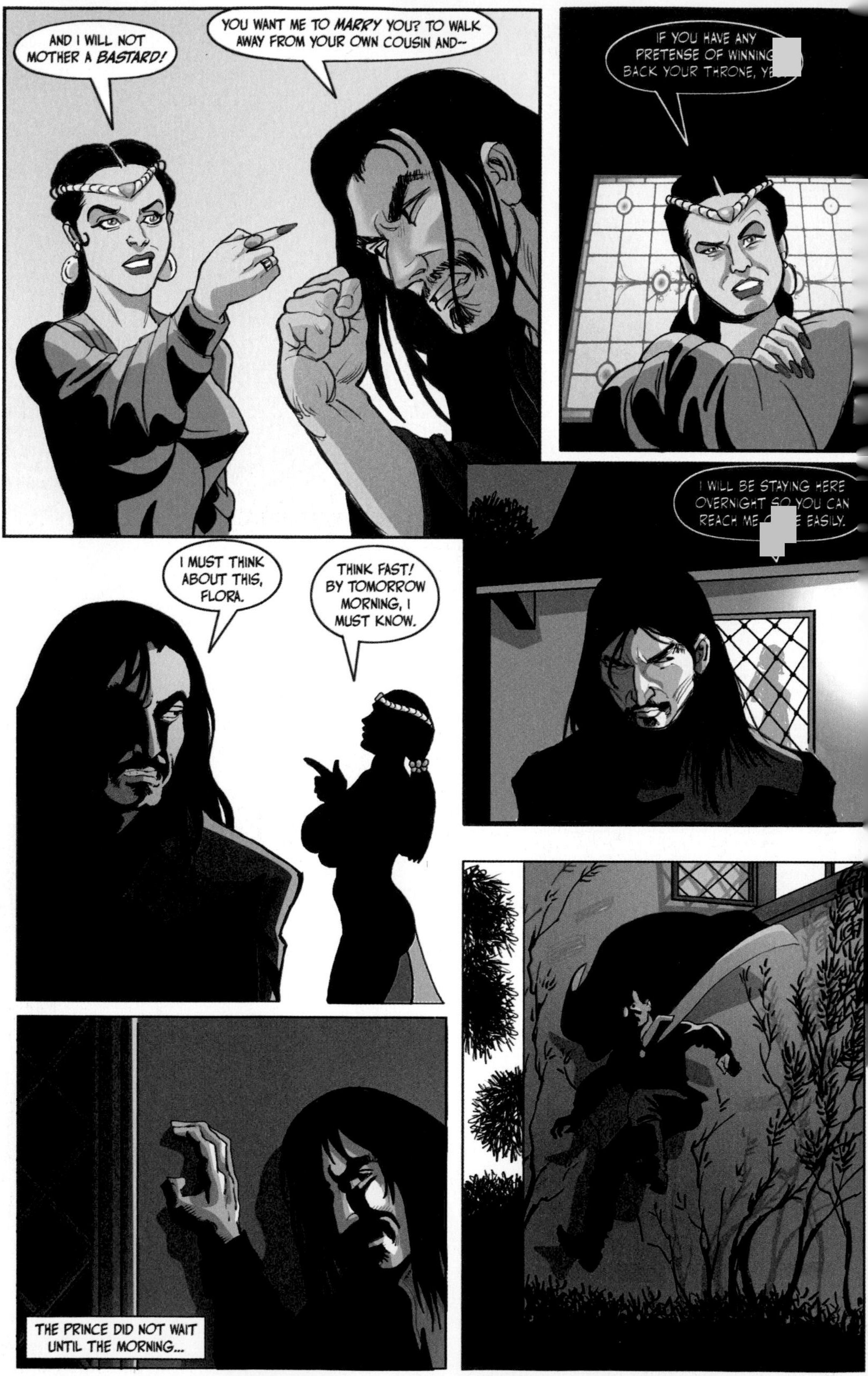
AND I WILL NOT MOTHER A *BASTARD!*
YOU WANT ME TO *MARRY* YOU? TO WALK AWAY FROM YOUR OWN COUSIN AND--
IF YOU HAVE ANY PRETENSE OF WINNING BACK YOUR THRONE, YE
I MUST THINK ABOUT THIS, FLORA.
THINK FAST! BY TOMORROW MORNING, I MUST KNOW.
I WILL BE STAYING HERE OVERNIGHT SO YOU CAN REACH ME EASILY.
THE PRINCE DID NOT WAIT UNTIL THE MORNING...

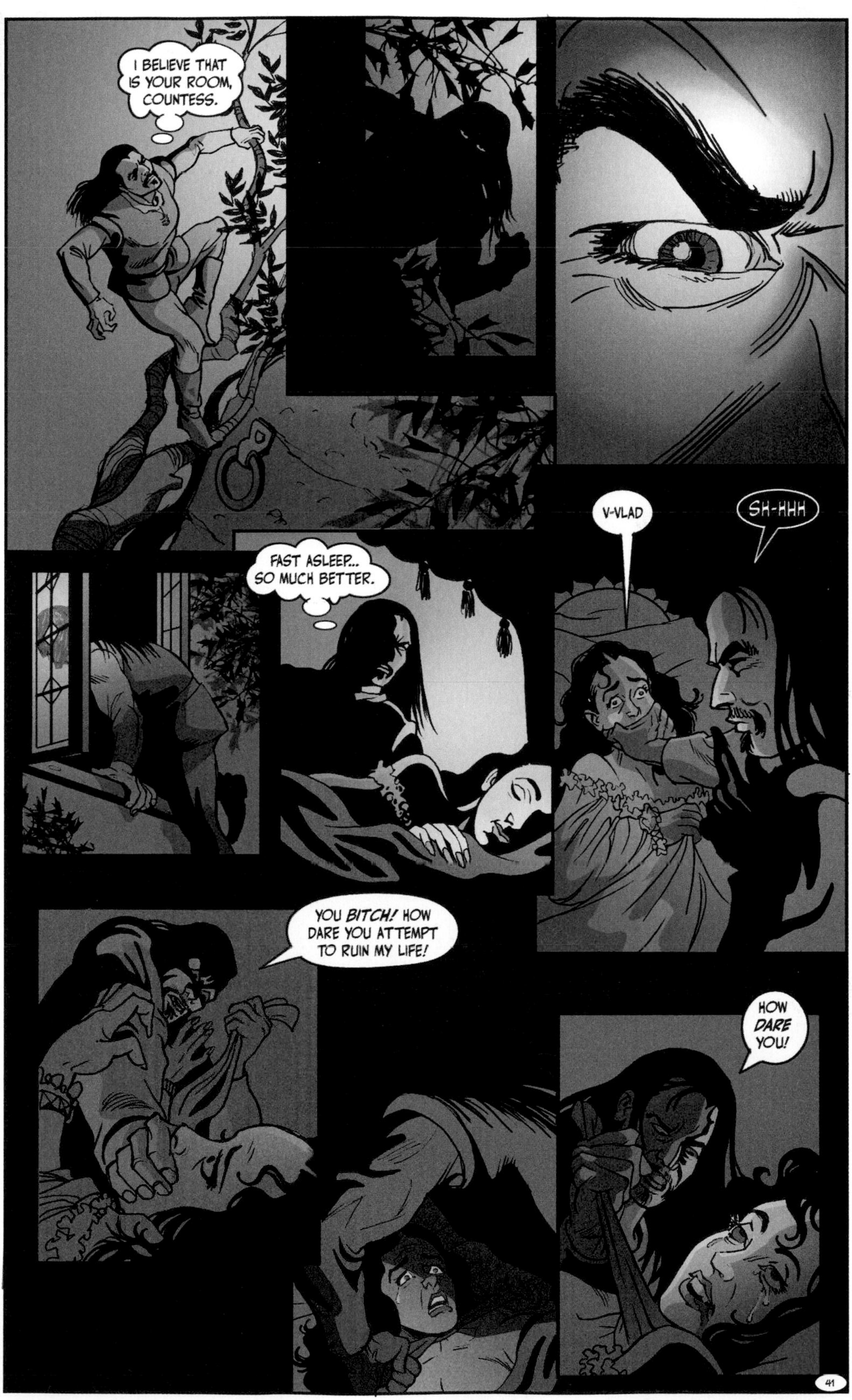
I BELIEVE THAT IS YOUR ROOM, COUNTESS.
FAST ASLEEP... SO MUCH BETTER.
V-VLAD
SH-HHH
YOU BITCH! HOW DARE YOU ATTEMPT TO RUIN MY LIFE!
HOW DARE YOU!

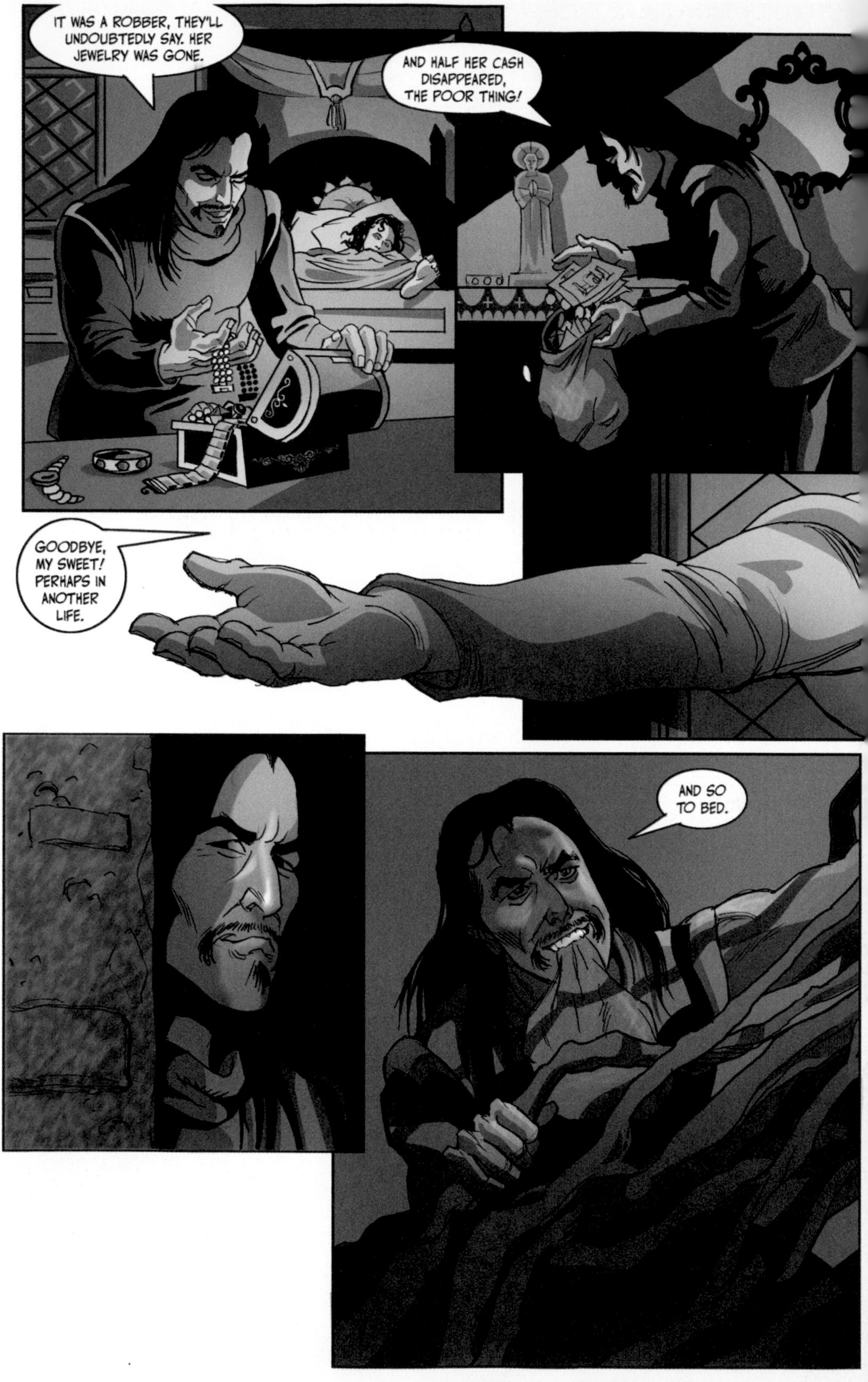
IT WAS A ROBBER, THEY'LL UNDOUBTEDLY SAY. HER JEWELRY WAS GONE.
AND HALF HER CASH DISAPPEARED, THE POOR THING!
GOODBYE, MY SWEET! PERHAPS IN ANOTHER LIFE.
AND SO TO BED.

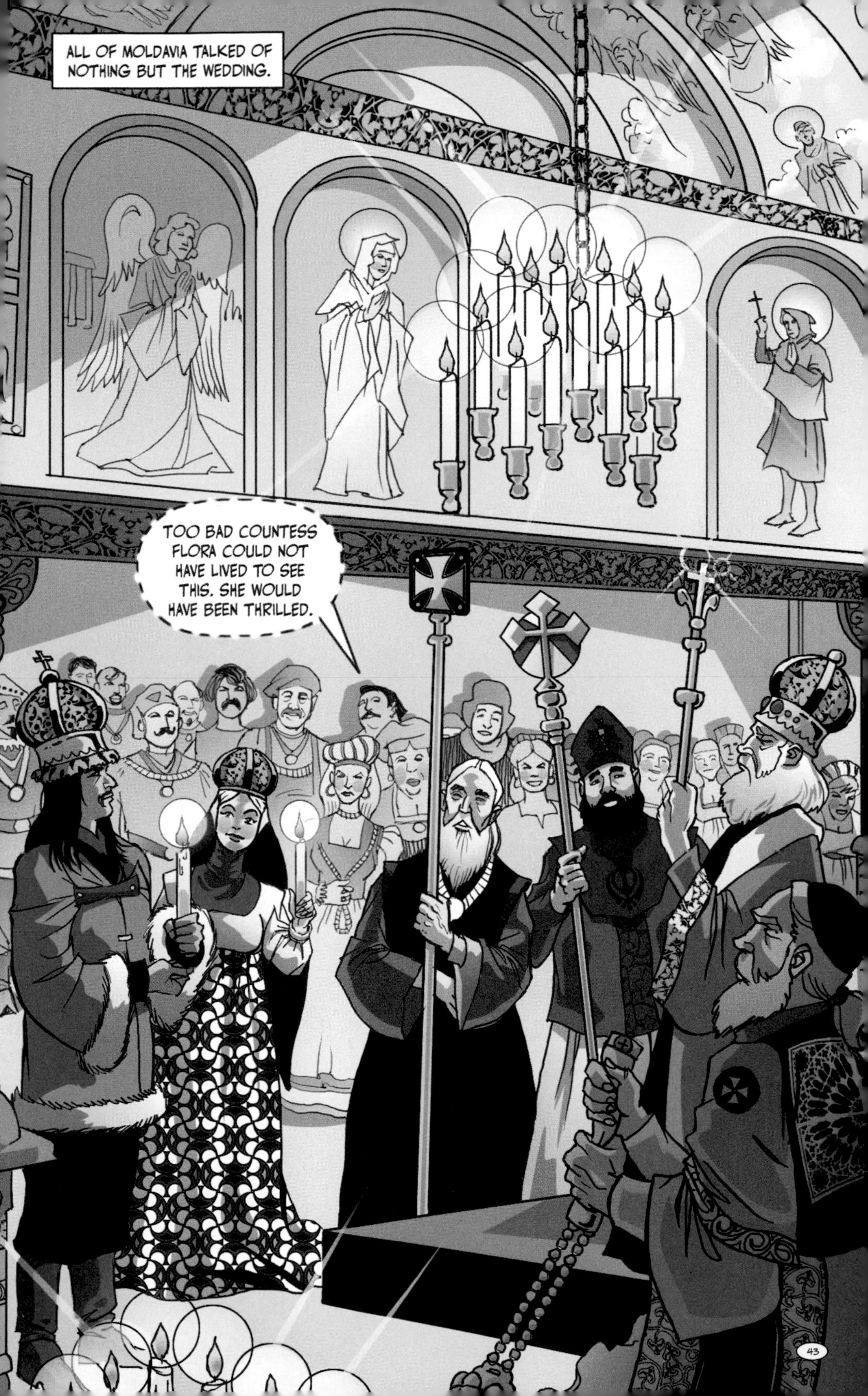
ALL OF MOLDAVIA TALKED OF NOTHING BUT THE WEDDING.
TOO BAD COUNTESS FLORA COULD NOT HAVE LIVED TO SEE THIS. SHE WOULD HAVE BEEN THRILLED.

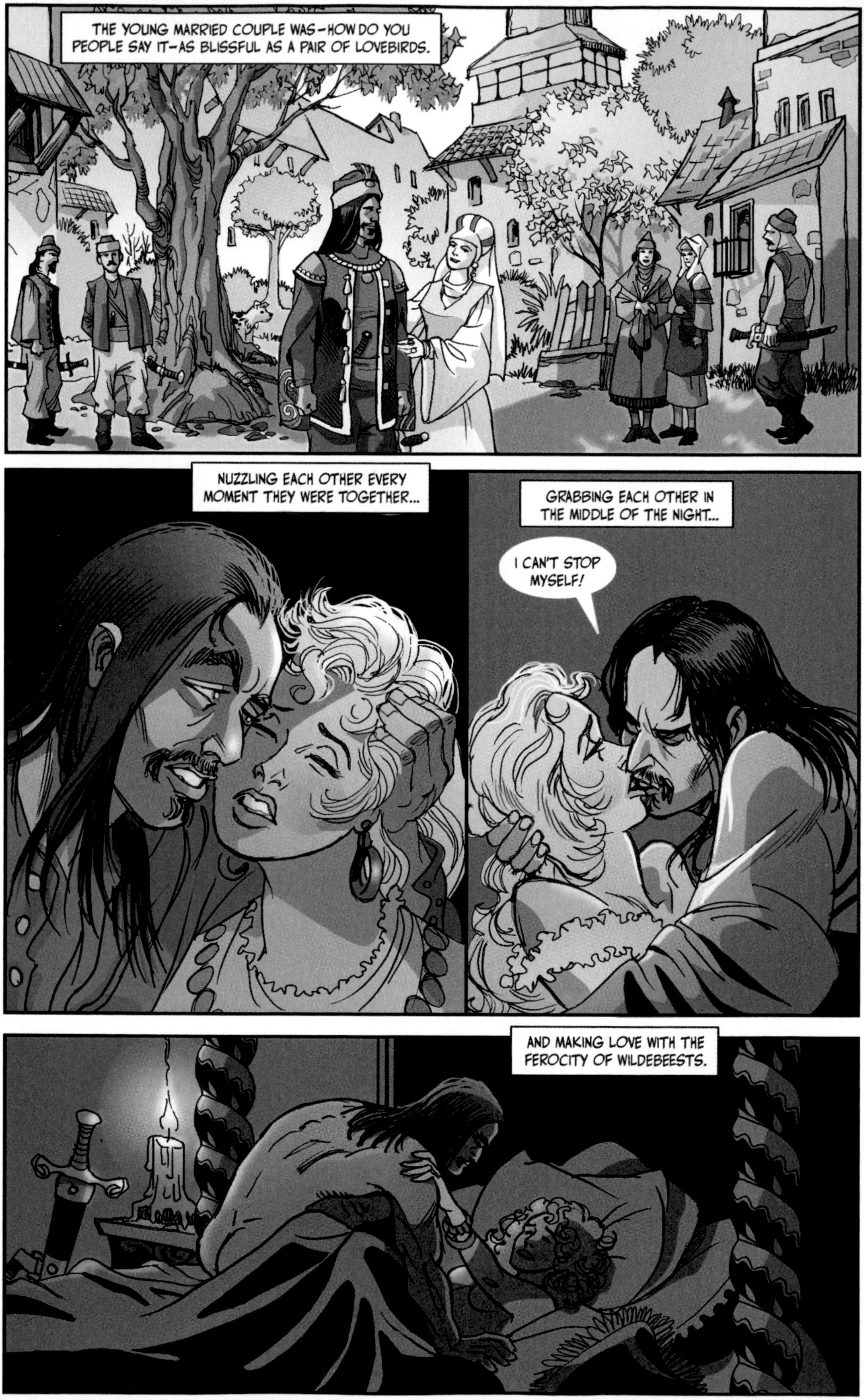
THE YOUNG MARRIED COUPLE WAS—HOW DO YOU PEOPLE SAY IT—AS BLISSFUL AS A PAIR OF LOVEBIRDS.
NUZZLING EACH OTHER EVERY MOMENT THEY WERE TOGETHER...
GRABBING EACH OTHER IN THE MIDDLE OF THE NIGHT...
I CAN'T STOP MYSELF!
AND MAKING LOVE WITH THE FEROCITY OF WILDEBEESTS.

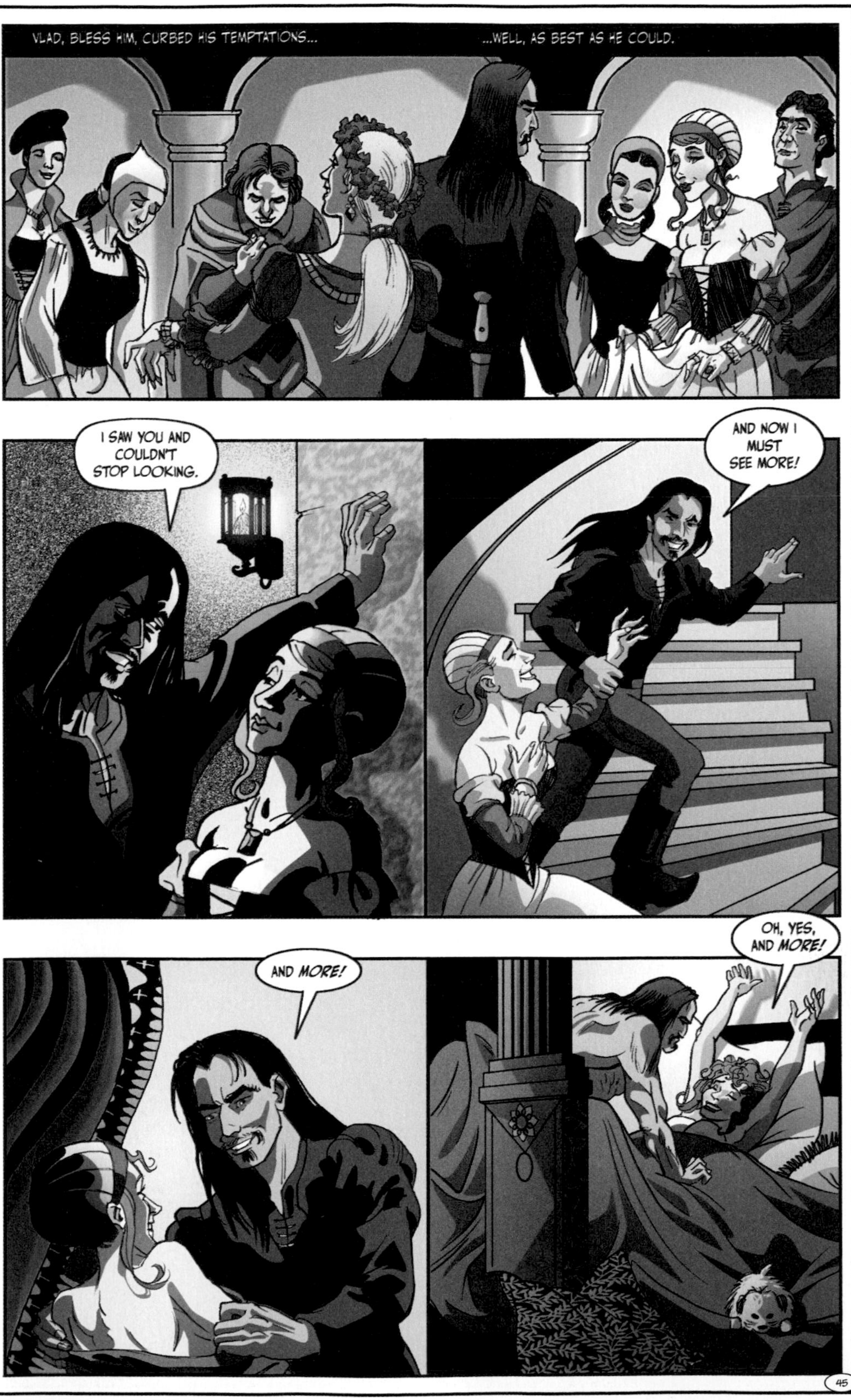
VLAD, BLESS HIM, CURBED HIS TEMPTATIONS...
...WELL, AS BEST AS HE COULD.
I SAW YOU AND COULDN'T STOP LOOKING.
AND NOW I MUST SEE MORE!
AND MORE!
OH, YES, AND MORE!

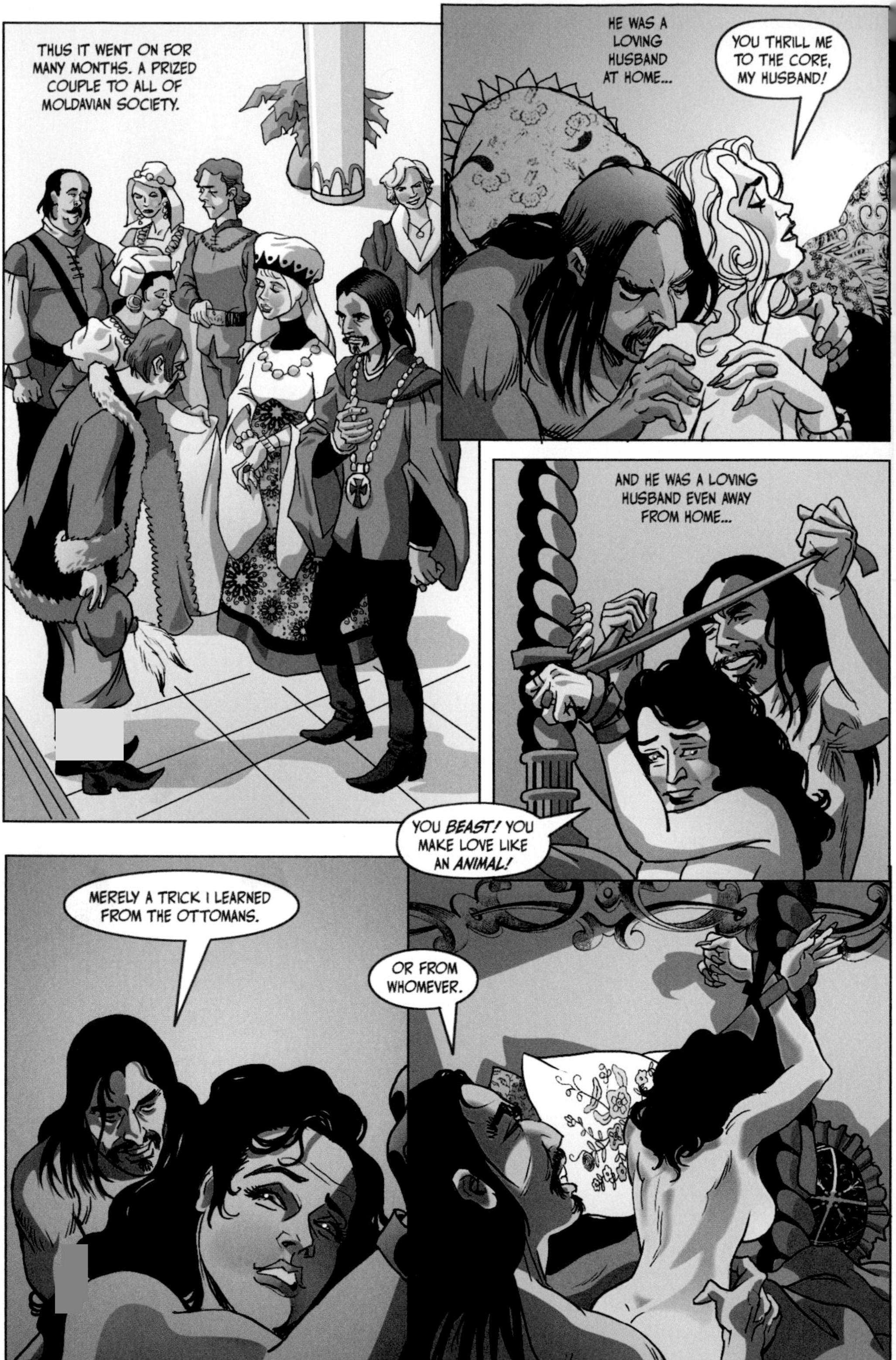

THUS IT WENT ON FOR MANY MONTHS. A PRIZED COUPLE TO ALL OF MOLDAVIAN SOCIETY.
HE WAS A LOVING HUSBAND AT HOME...
YOU THRILL ME TO THE CORE, MY HUSBAND!
AND HE WAS A LOVING HUSBAND EVEN AWAY FROM HOME...
YOU BEAST! YOU MAKE LOVE LIKE AN ANIMAL!
MERELY A TRICK I LEARNED FROM THE OTTOMANS.
OR FROM WHOMEVER.

SOMETIME AFTER, VLAD WAS ASKED TO ATTEND A MEETING OF A GROUP OF MOLDAVIAN NOBLEMEN...

AH, PRINCE VLAD, WE ARE SO GLAD YOU COULD JOIN US.

I AM HONORED, SIR.

IS THERE PERHAPS SOME REASON I AM HERE?

WE WILL SPEAK FRANKLY, PRINCE, MANY OF US HAVE BEEN DISAPPOINTED BY THE ACTIONS OF THE PRESENT REGIME IN YOUR NATIVE LAND. THEY PAY US NO ATTENTION AND--

ALLOW *ME* TO SPEAK!

I AM PRINCE GARACH OF BULGARIA, MY FRIEND. AND WE ARE MORE THAN DISAPPOINTED. WE HAVE BEEN *DISGRACED* BY THIS VLADISLOV, WHO RULES WALLACHIA.

HE IS A CHICKEN WITH A MAN'S HEAD.

WE ARE LOOKING FOR A MAN WITH THE BALLS OF A LION, AND ONE WHO WILL LOOK *OUR* WAY!

I HAVE NOT EXAMINED MYSELF LATELY, GENTLEMEN, BUT IF YOU BELIEVE I POSSESS SUCH AN ENDOWMENT...

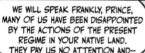

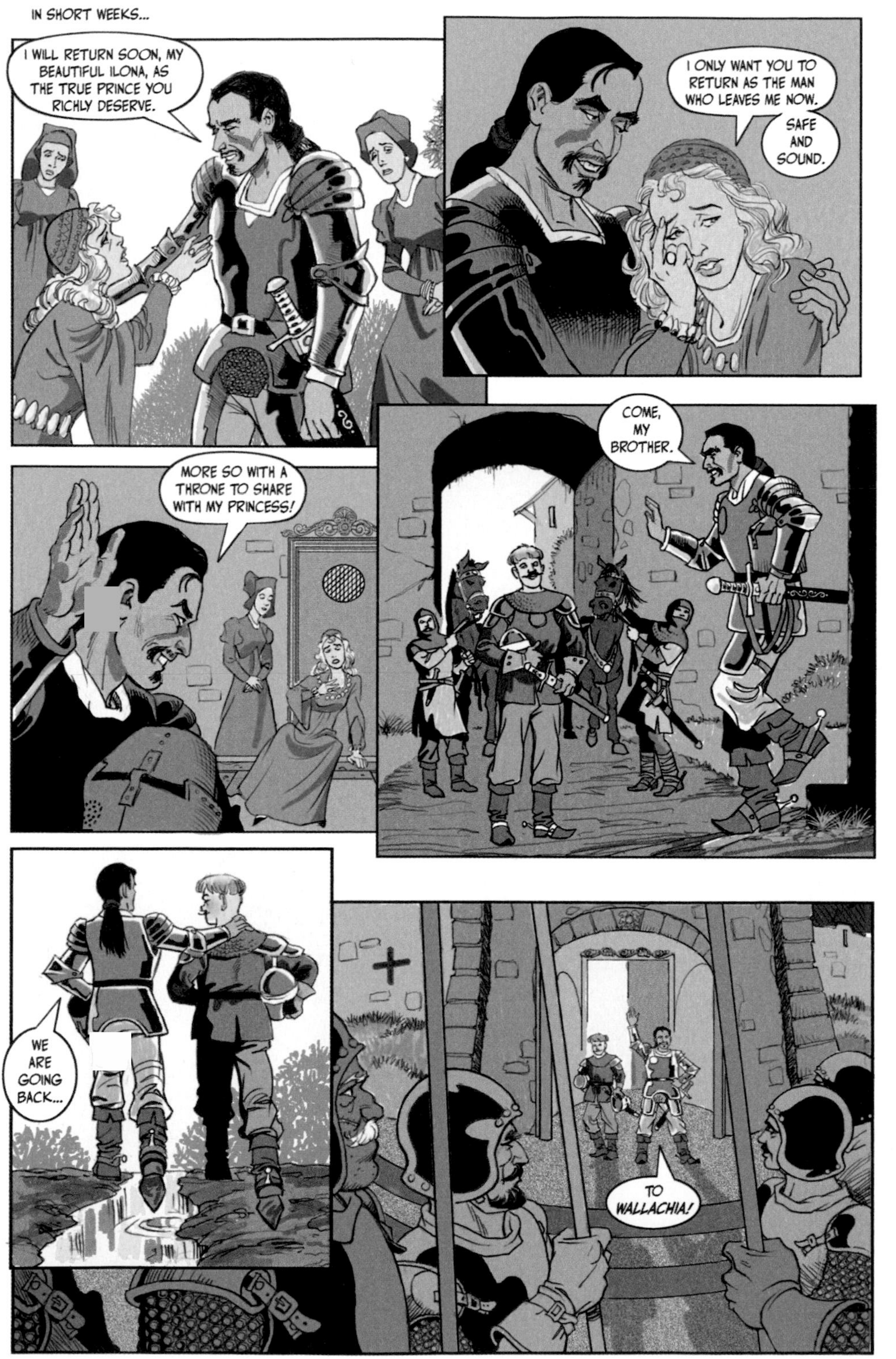
IN SHORT WEEKS...
I WILL RETURN SOON, MY BEAUTIFUL ILONA, AS THE TRUE PRINCE YOU RICHLY DESERVE.
I ONLY WANT YOU TO RETURN AS THE MAN WHO LEAVES ME NOW.
SAFE AND SOUND.
MORE SO WITH A THRONE TO SHARE WITH MY PRINCESS!
COME, MY BROTHER.
WE ARE GOING BACK...
TO WALLACHIA!

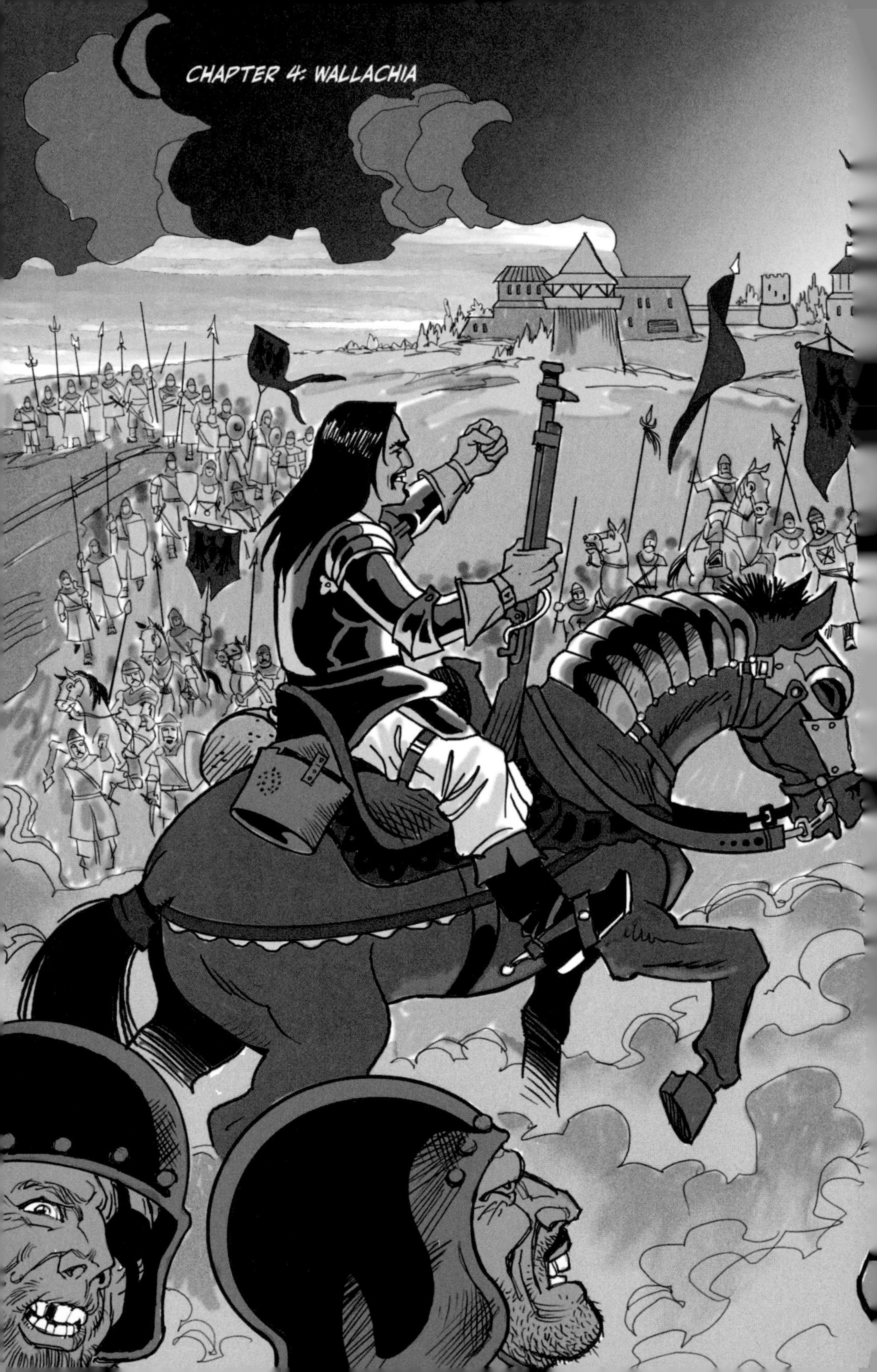
CHAPTER 4: WALLACHIA

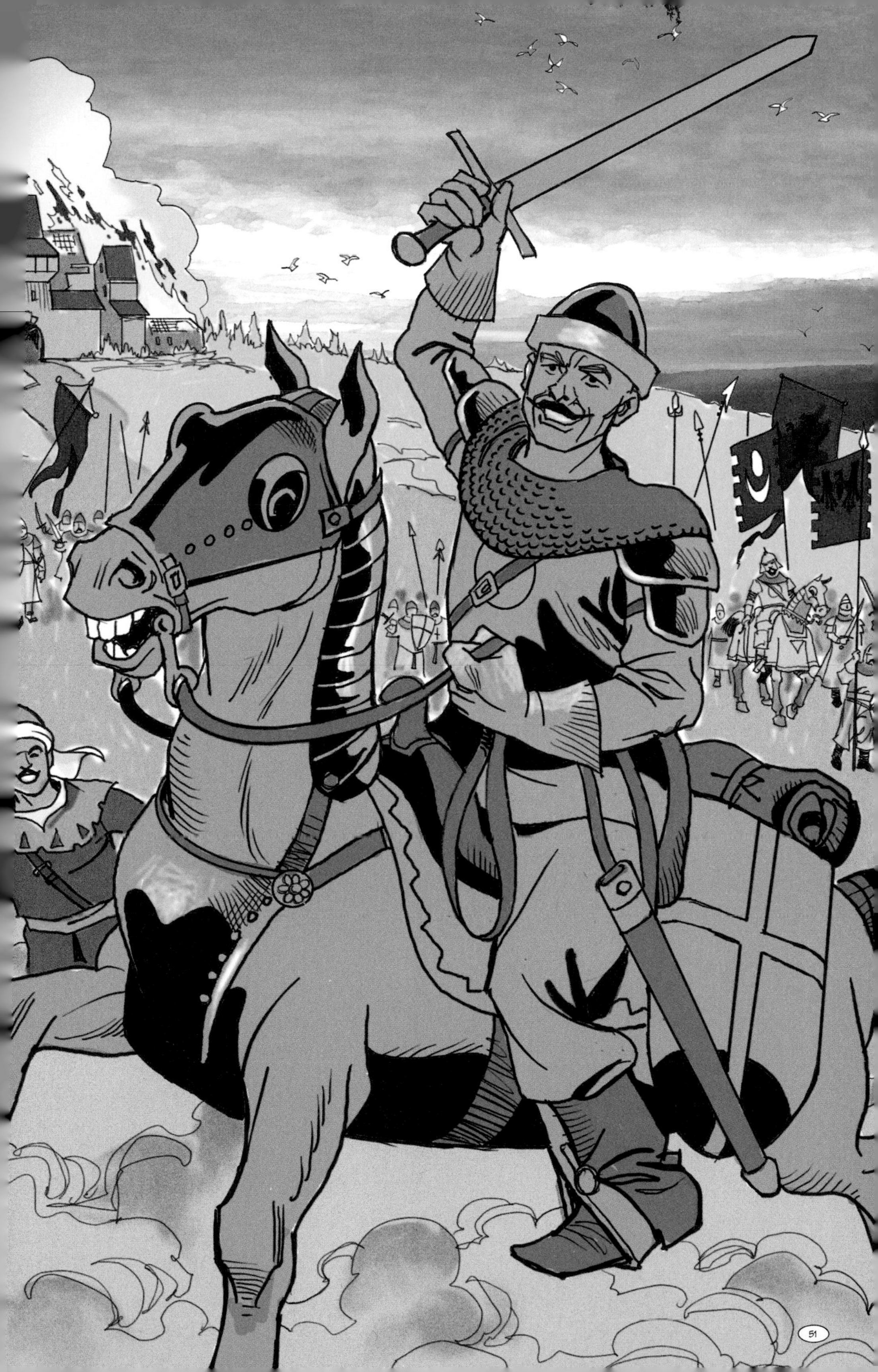

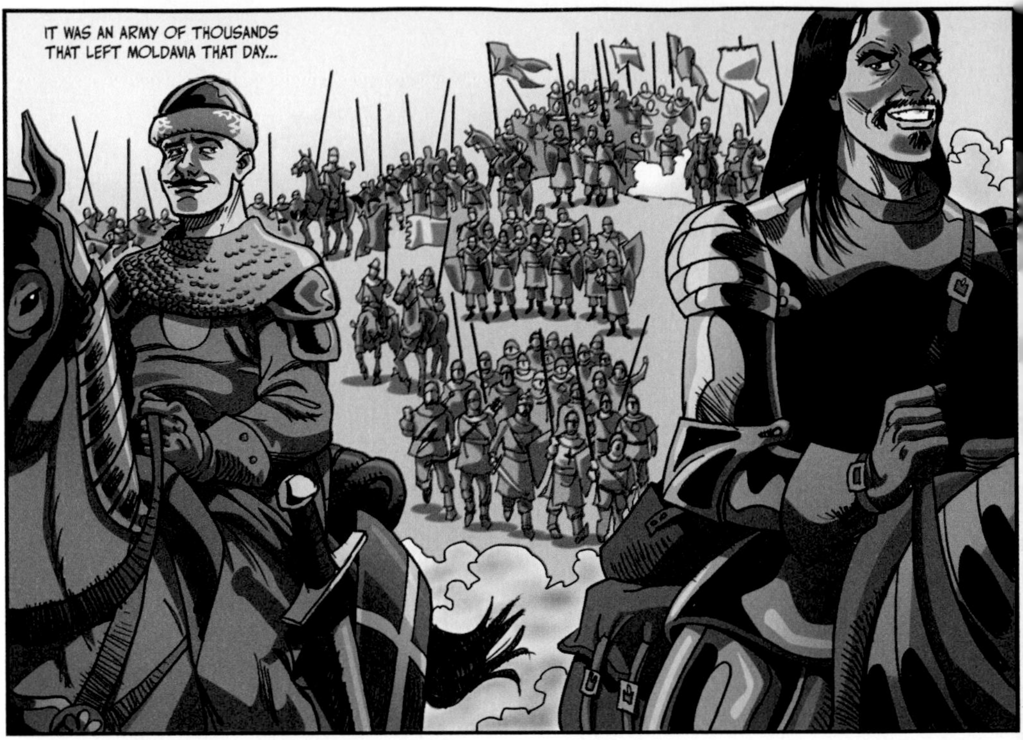
IT WAS AN ARMY OF THOUSANDS THAT LEFT MOLDAVIA THAT DAY...

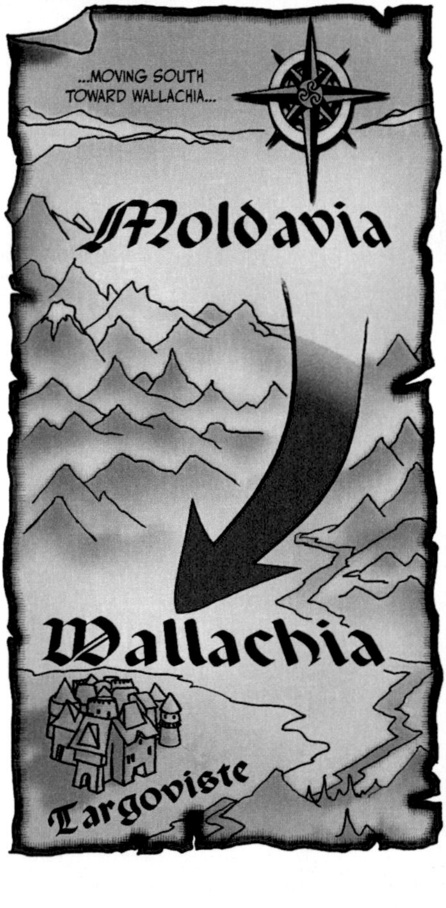
...MOVING SOUTH TOWARD WALLACHIA...
Moldavia
Wallachia
Targoviste

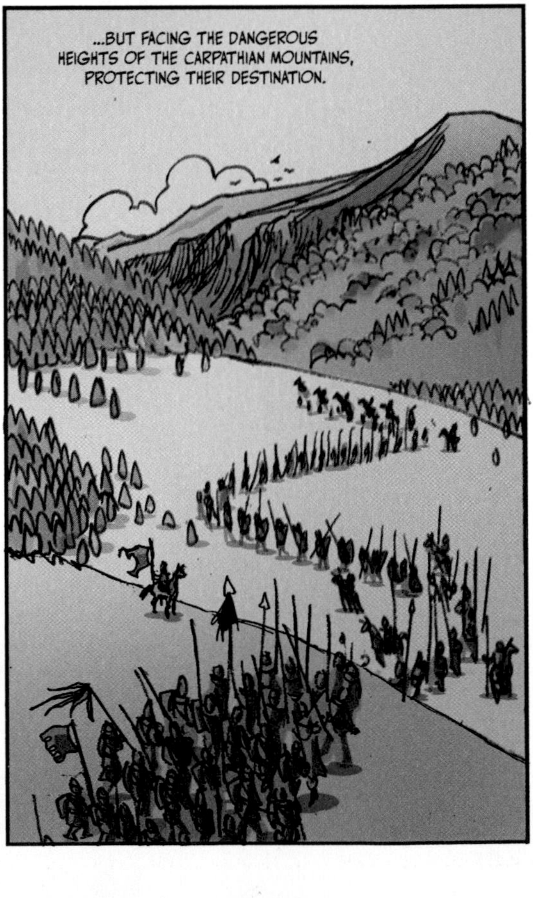
...BUT FACING THE DANGEROUS HEIGHTS OF THE CARPATHIAN MOUNTAINS, PROTECTING THEIR DESTINATION.

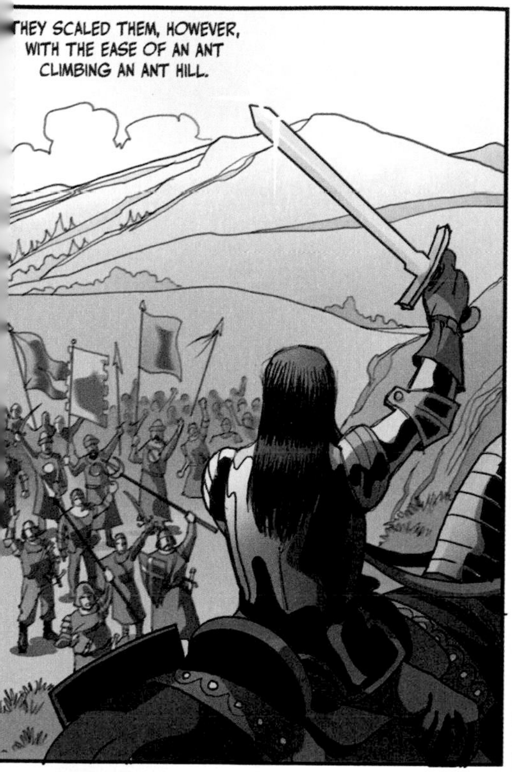
THEY SCALED THEM, HOWEVER, WITH THE EASE OF AN ANT CLIMBING AN ANT HILL.

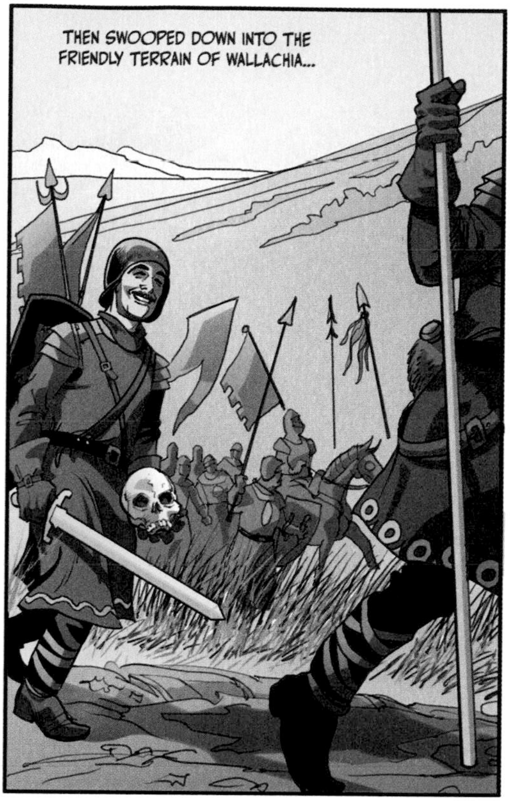
THEN SWOOPED DOWN INTO THE FRIENDLY TERRAIN OF WALLACHIA...

...WHERE THEY SWEPT THROUGH CITY AFTER CITY...

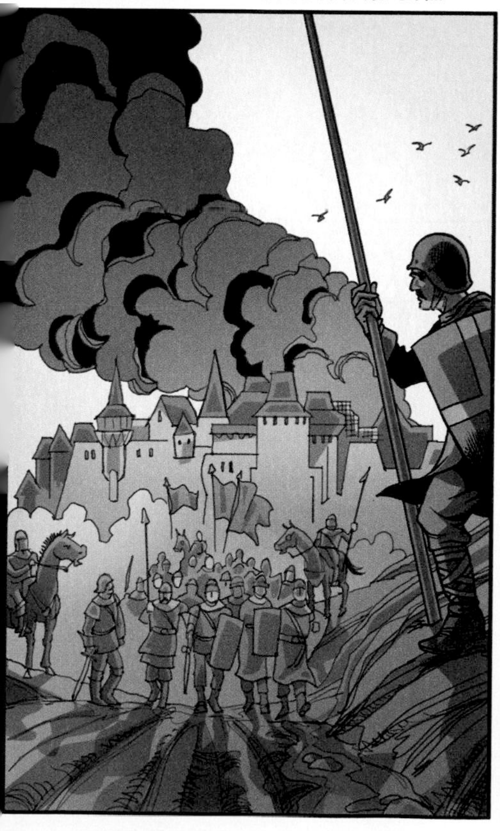

...LEAVING BLOOD IN THEIR TRACKS AND THE SMELL OF VICTORY IN THEIR NOSTRILS.

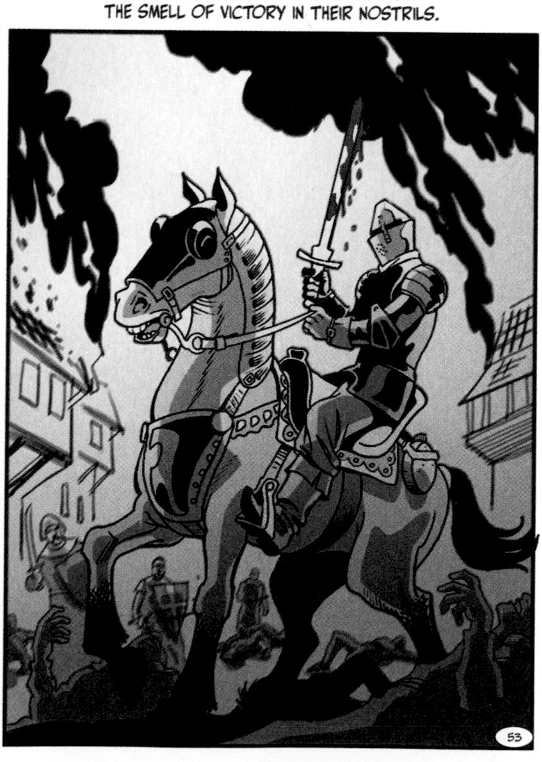

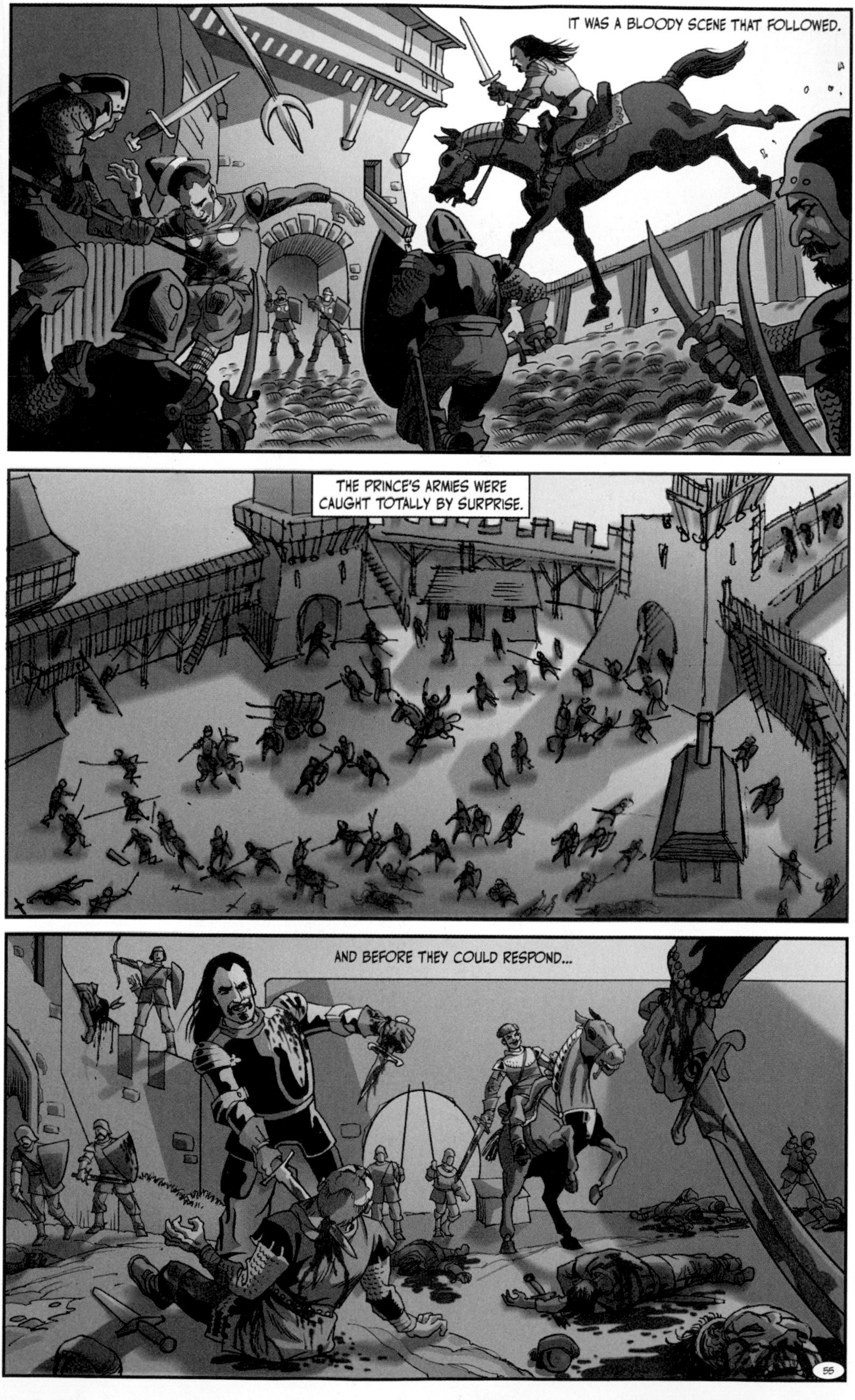
IT WAS A BLOODY SCENE THAT FOLLOWED.
THE PRINCE'S ARMIES WERE CAUGHT TOTALLY BY SURPRISE.
AND BEFORE THEY COULD RESPOND...

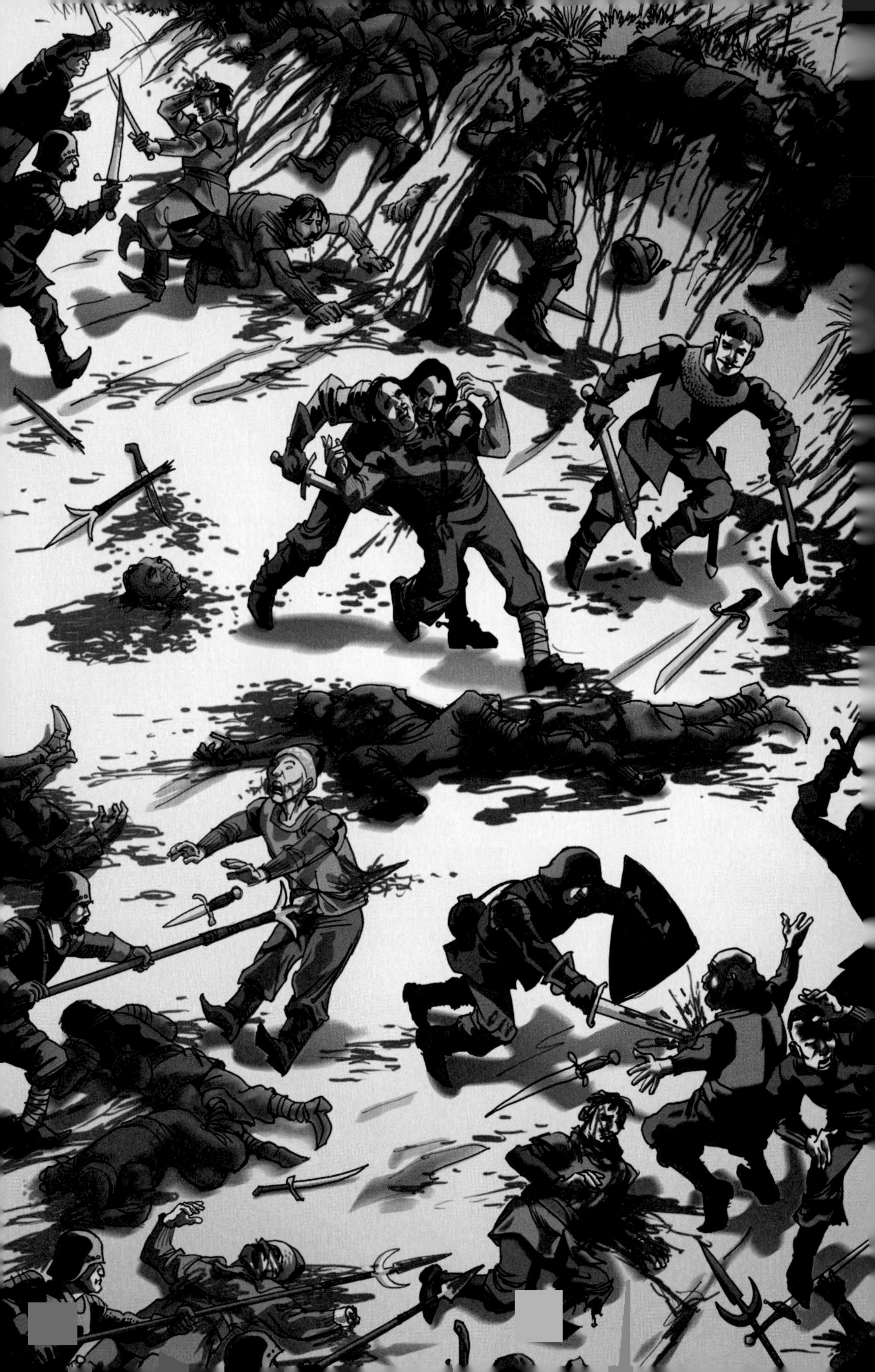

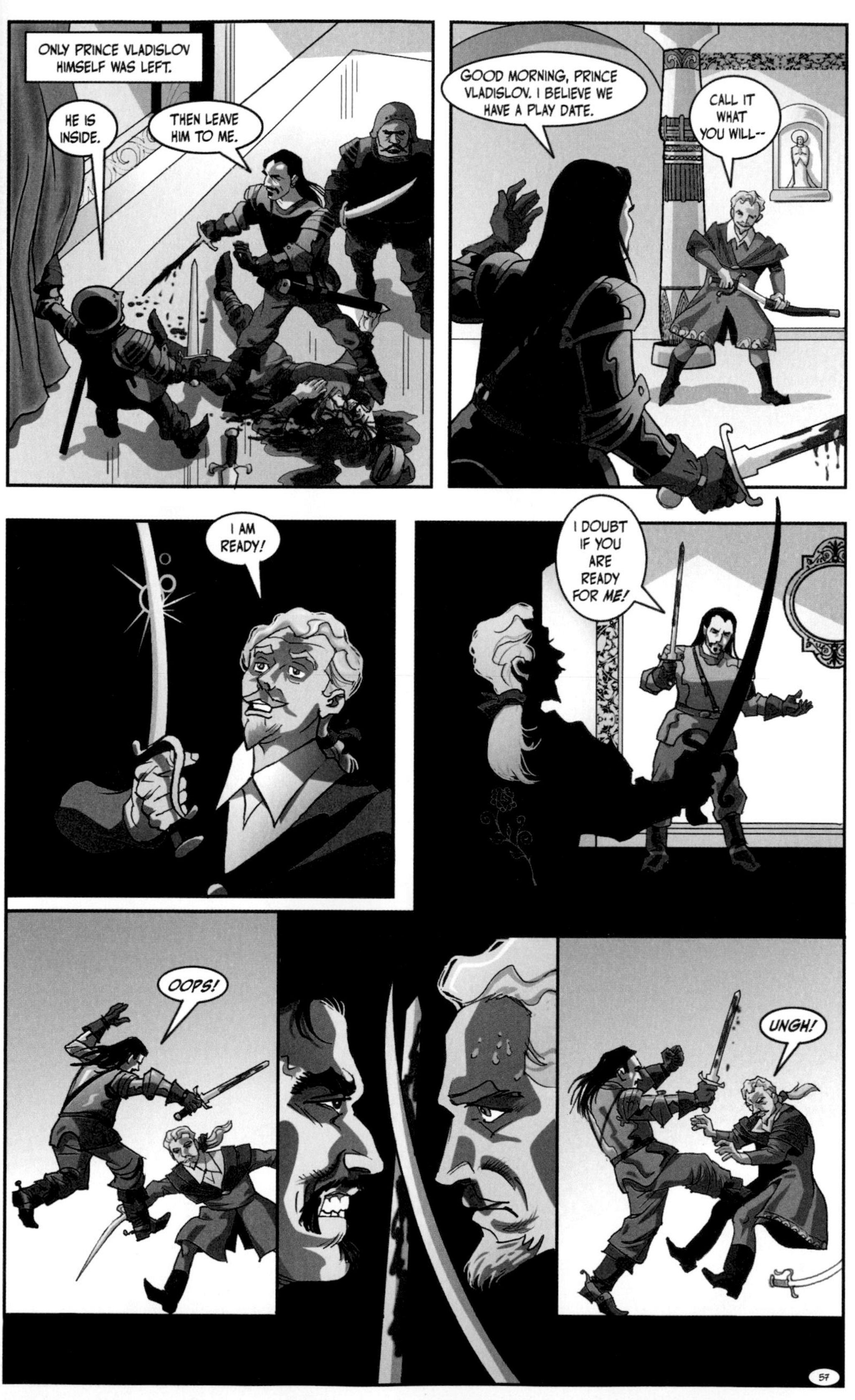
ONLY PRINCE VLADISLOV HIMSELF WAS LEFT.
HE IS INSIDE.
THEN LEAVE HIM TO ME.
GOOD MORNING, PRINCE VLADISLOV. I BELIEVE WE HAVE A PLAY DATE.
CALL IT WHAT YOU WILL--
I AM READY!
I DOUBT IF YOU ARE READY FOR *ME!*
OOPS!
UNGH!

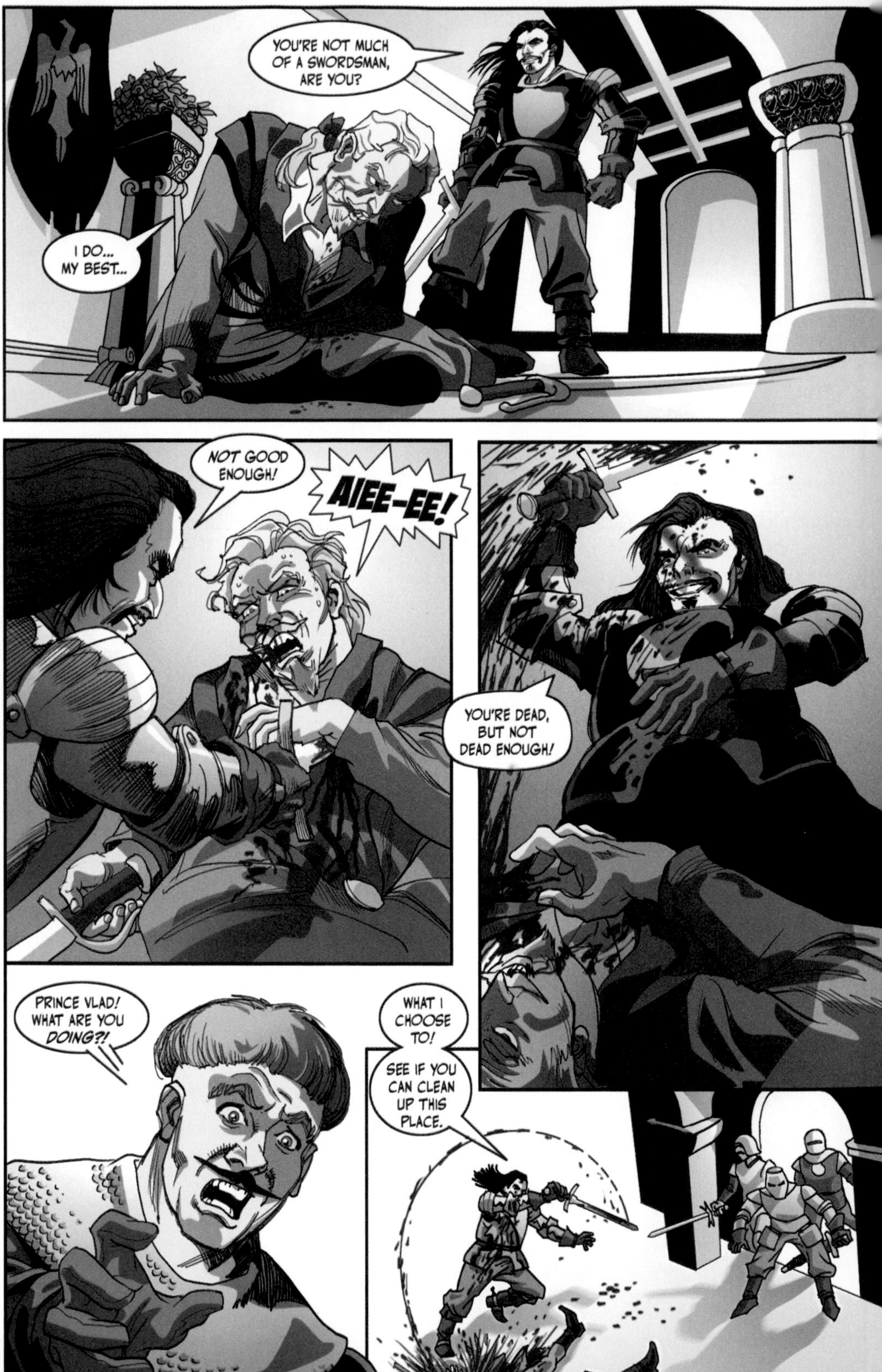
YOU'RE NOT MUCH OF A SWORDSMAN, ARE YOU?
I DO... MY BEST...
NOT GOOD ENOUGH!
AIEE-EE!
YOU'RE DEAD, BUT NOT DEAD ENOUGH!
PRINCE VLAD! WHAT ARE YOU DOING?!
WHAT I CHOOSE TO!
SEE IF YOU CAN CLEAN UP THIS PLACE.

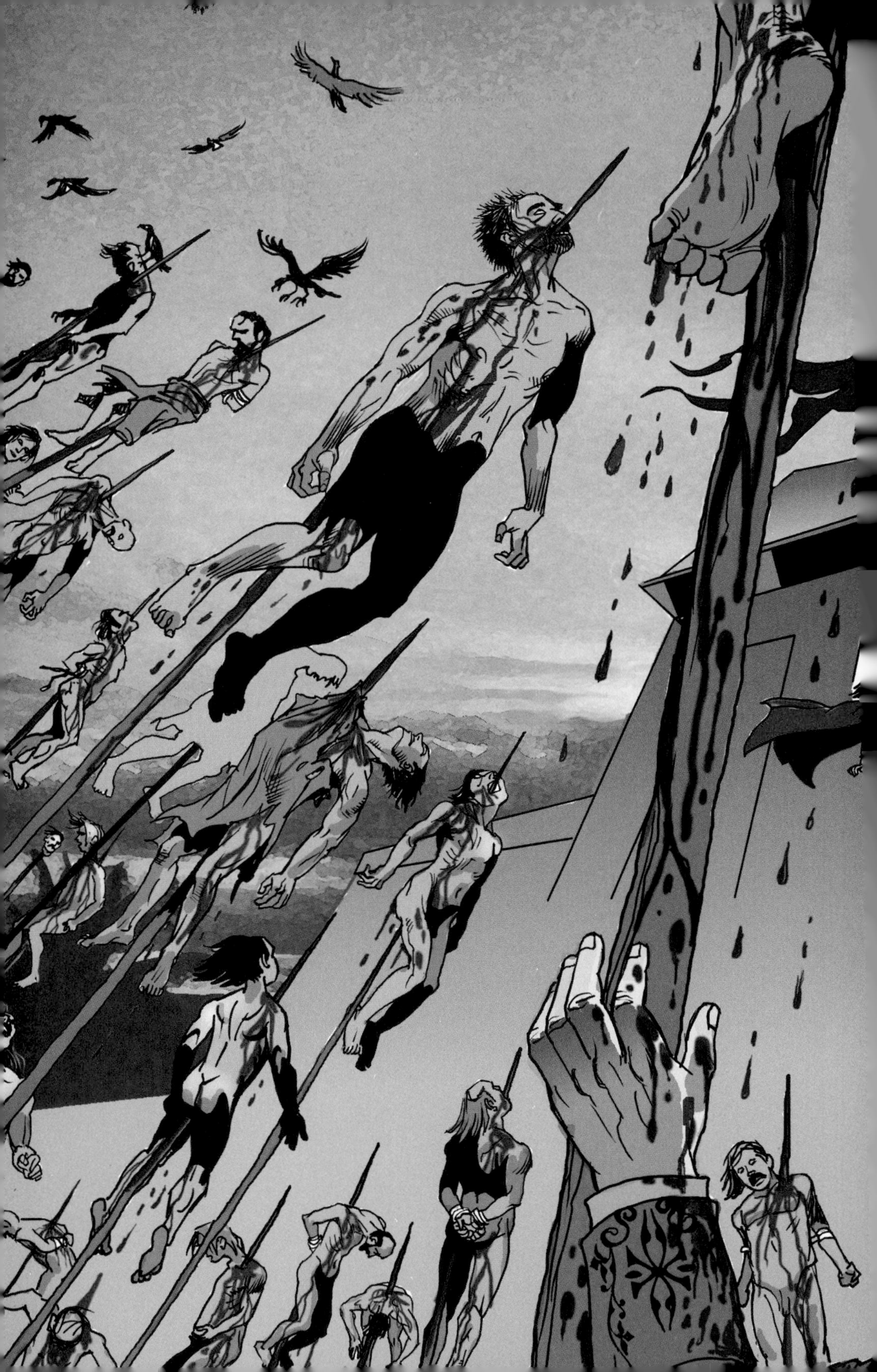

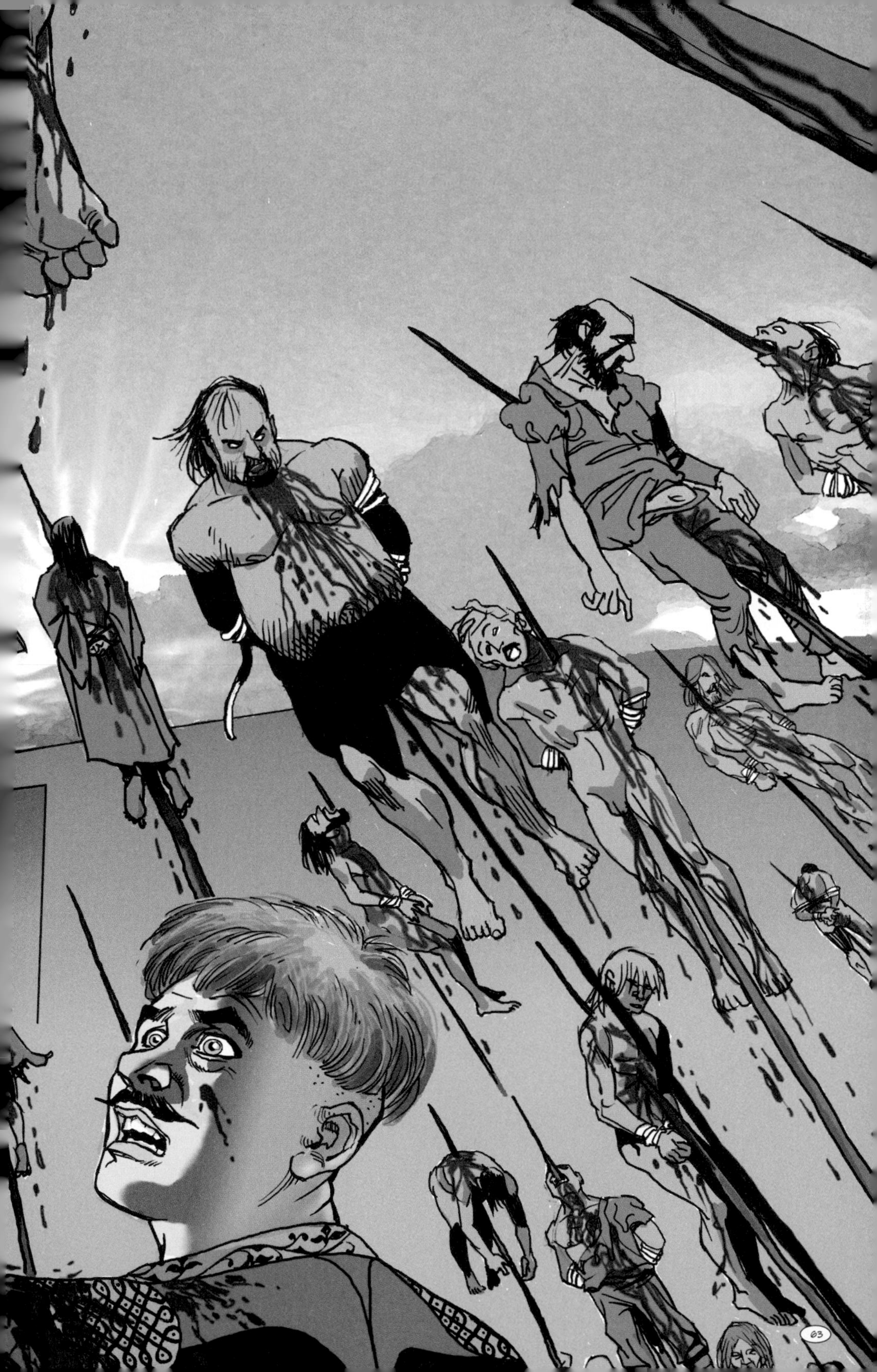

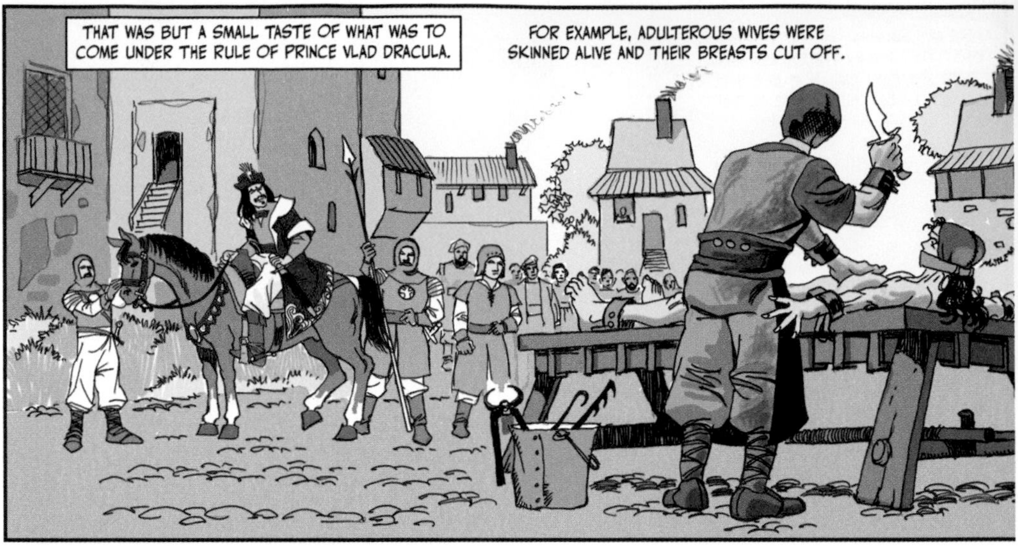
THAT WAS BUT A SMALL TASTE OF WHAT WAS TO COME UNDER THE RULE OF PRINCE VLAD DRACULA.
FOR EXAMPLE, ADULTEROUS WIVES WERE SKINNED ALIVE AND THEIR BREASTS CUT OFF.

RELIGIOUS MEN WHO WOULDN'T REMOVE THEIR HATS...

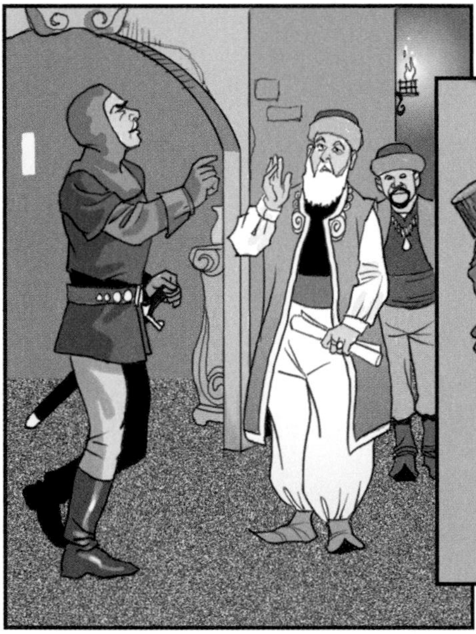

...HAD THEM NAILED ONTO THEIR SKULLS.

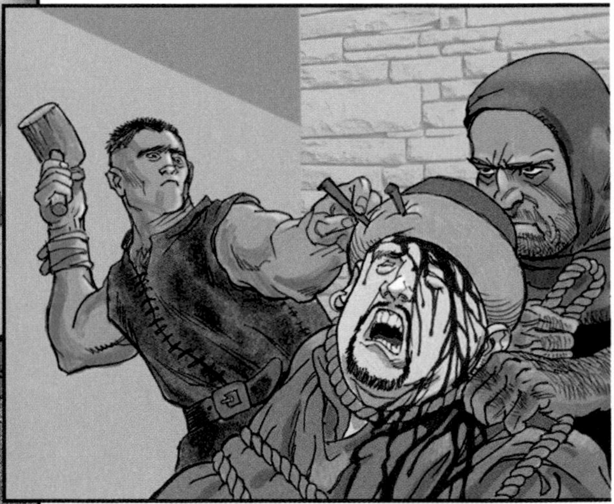

A ROOMFUL OF BEGGARS WERE FED LIKE THEY NEVER HAD BEEN BEFORE...

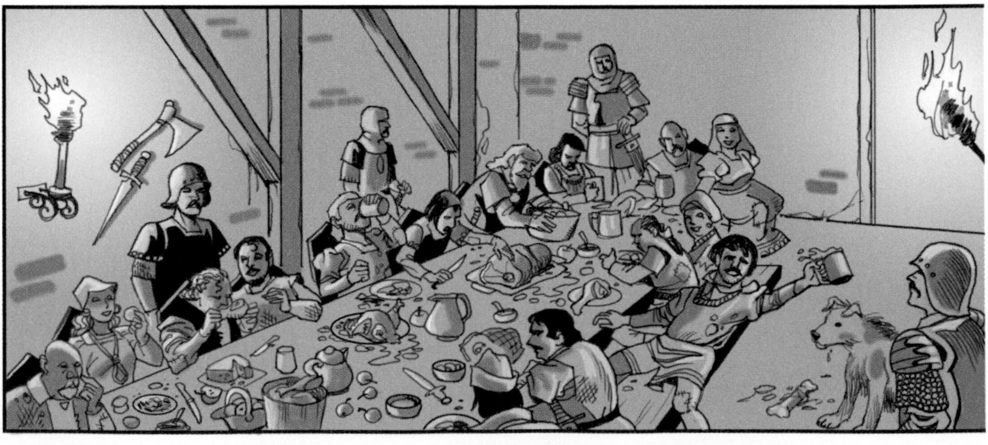

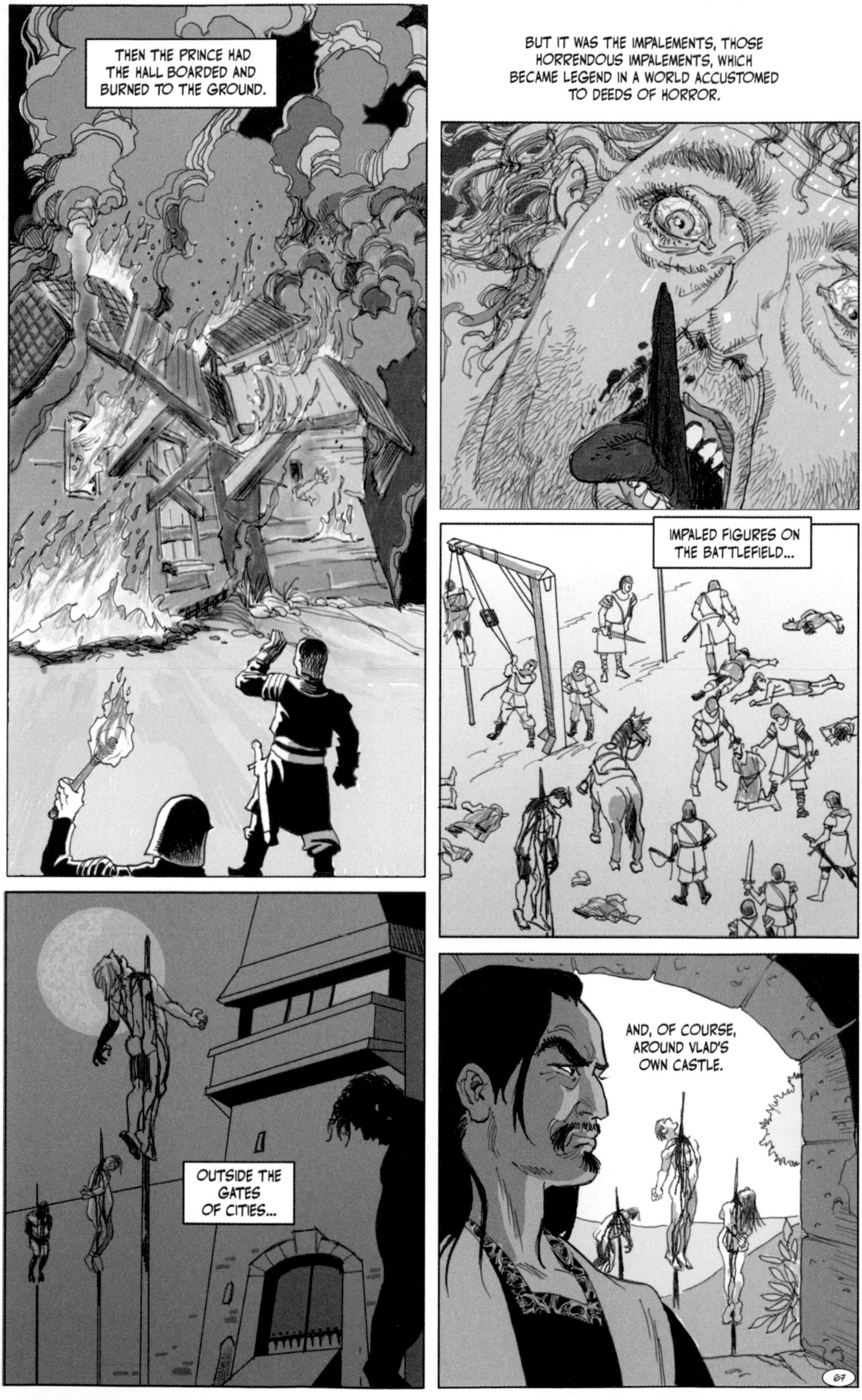
THEN THE PRINCE HAD THE HALL BOARDED AND BURNED TO THE GROUND.
BUT IT WAS THE IMPALEMENTS, THOSE HORRENDOUS IMPALEMENTS, WHICH BECAME LEGEND IN A WORLD ACCUSTOMED TO DEEDS OF HORROR.
IMPALED FIGURES ON THE BATTLEFIELD...
OUTSIDE THE GATES OF CITIES...
AND, OF COURSE, AROUND VLAD'S OWN CASTLE.

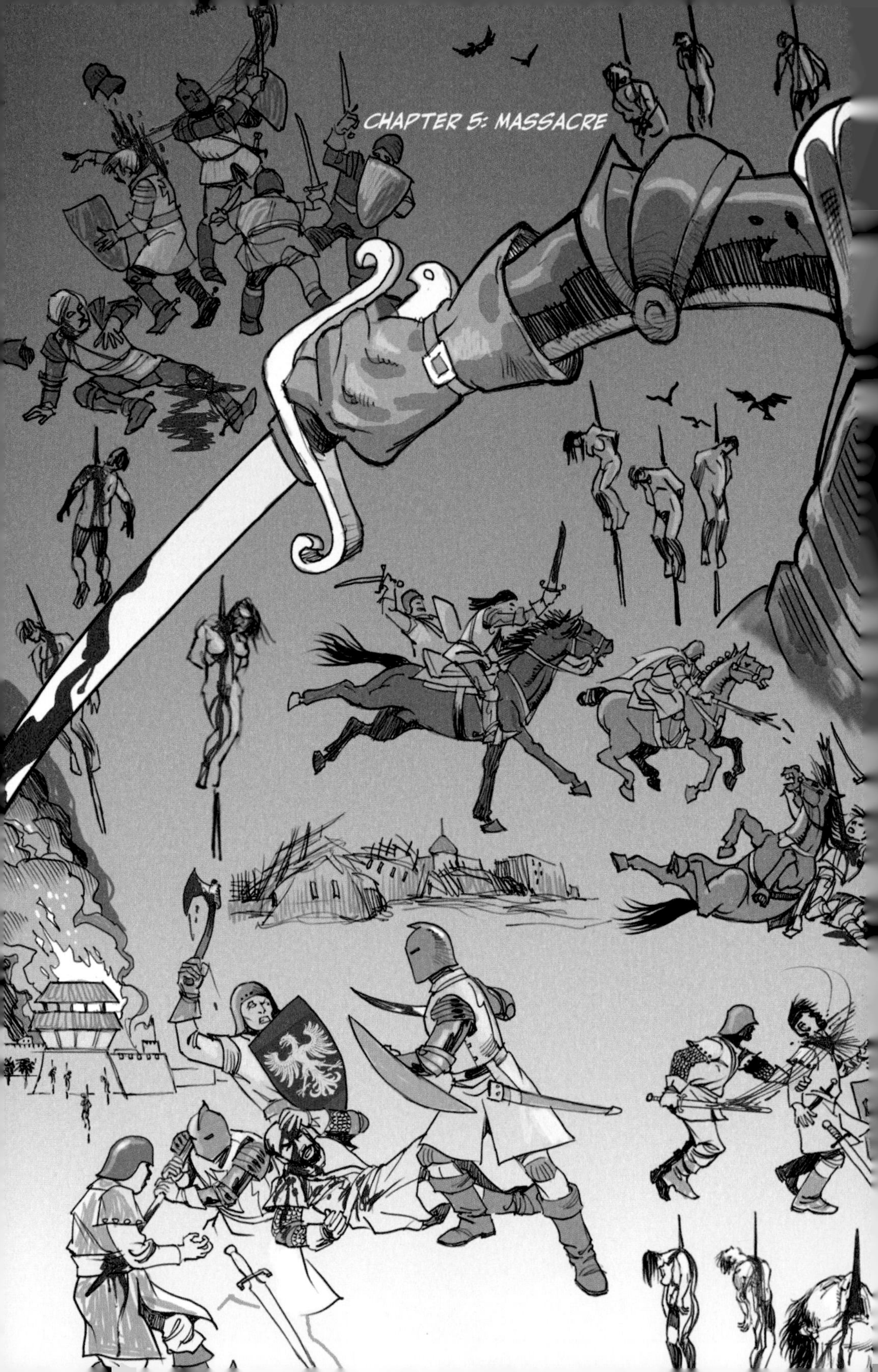
CHAPTER 5: MASSACRE

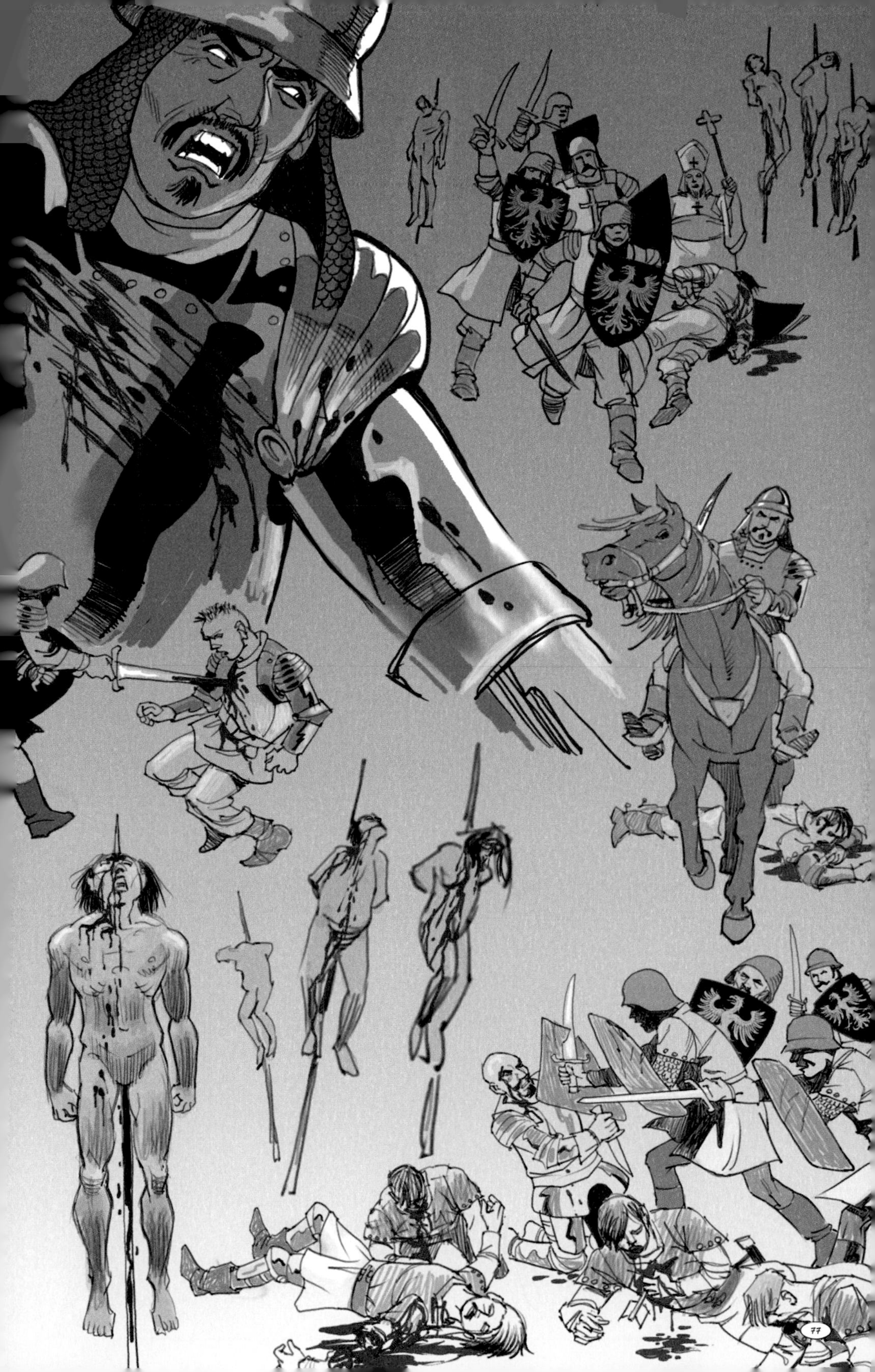

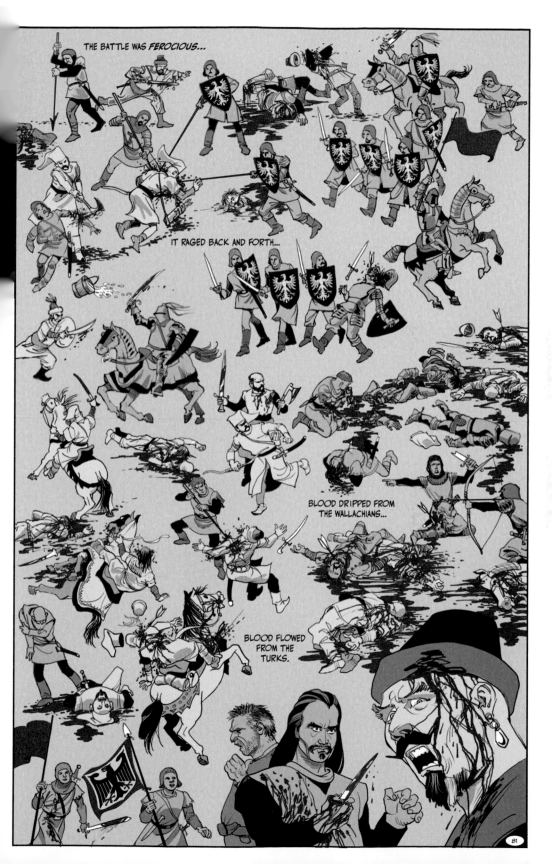

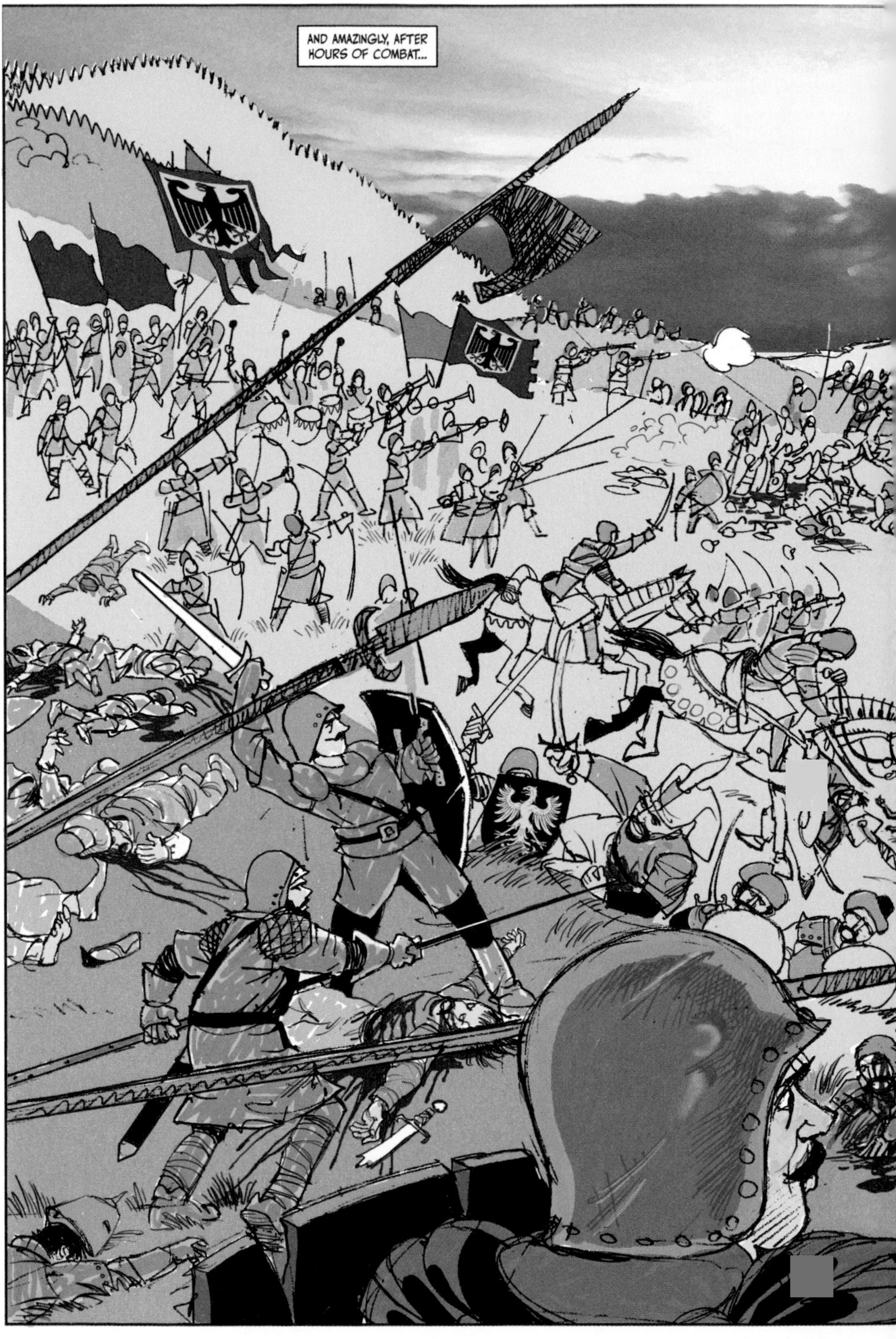
AND AMAZINGLY, AFTER HOURS OF COMBAT...

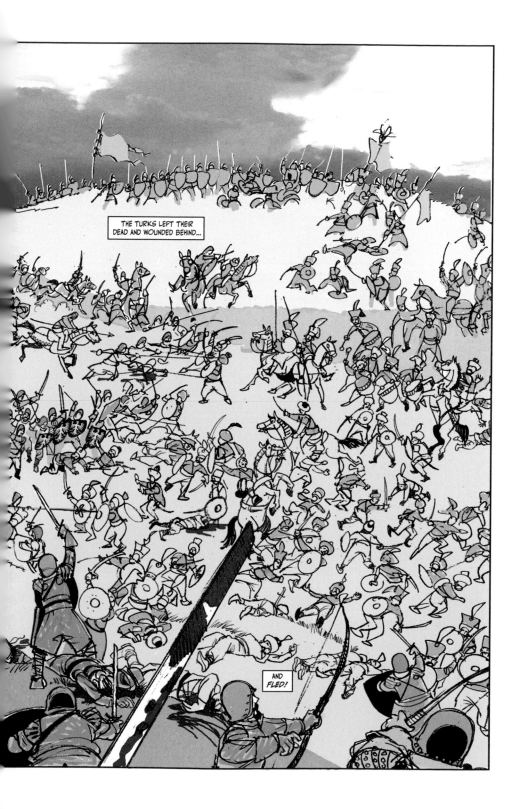

CHAPTER 6: BROTHERS

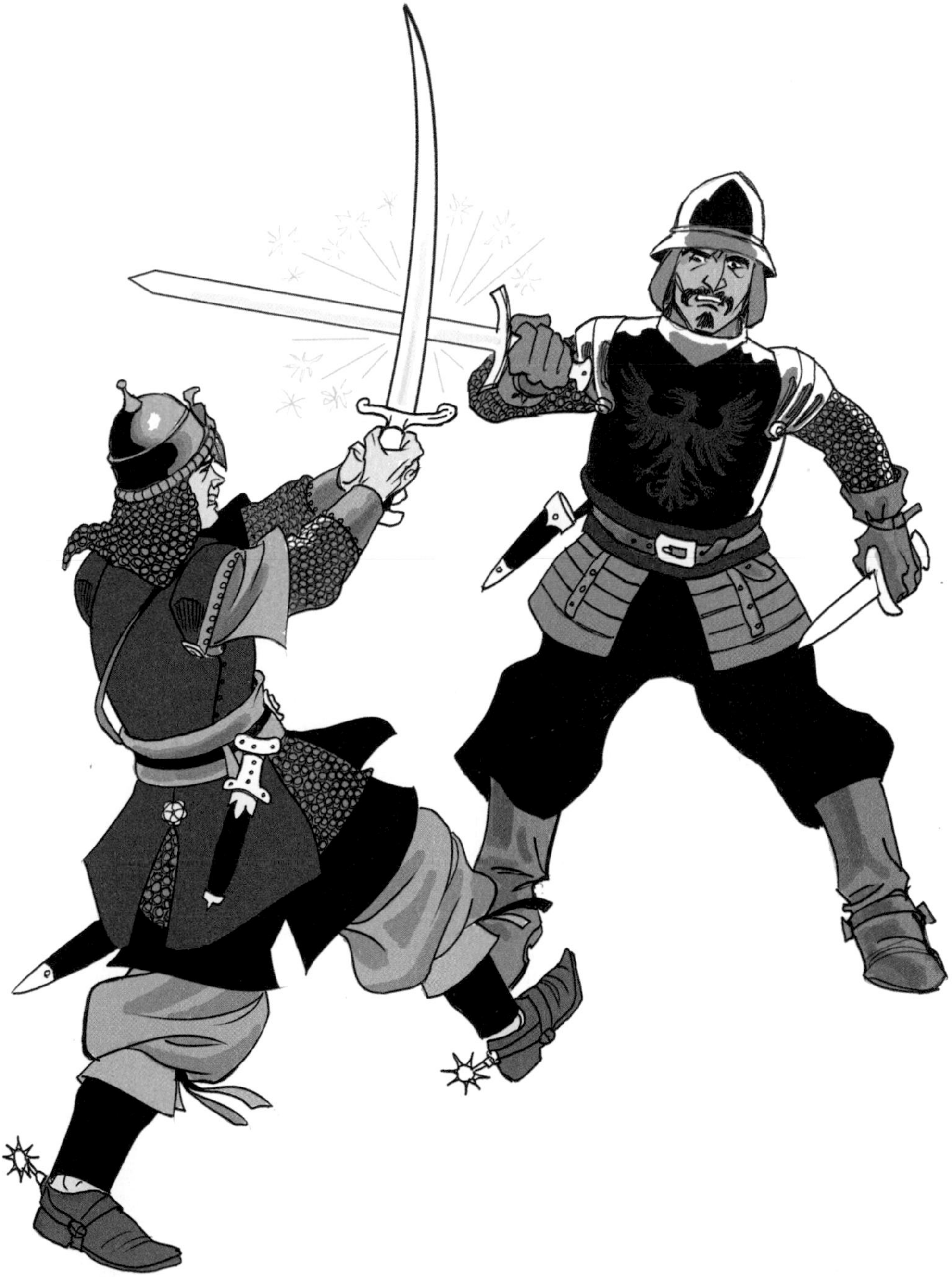

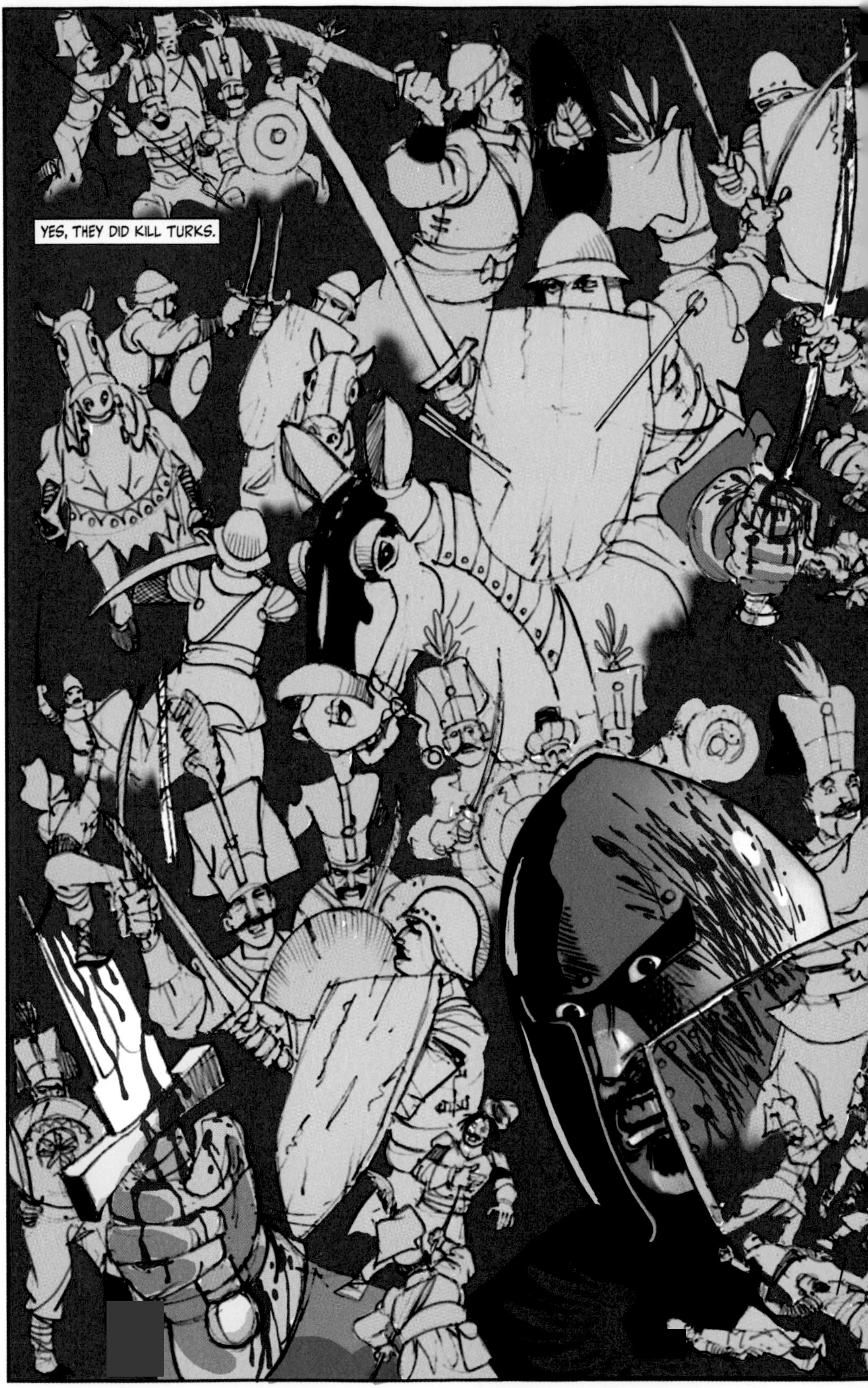
YES, THEY DID KILL TURKS.

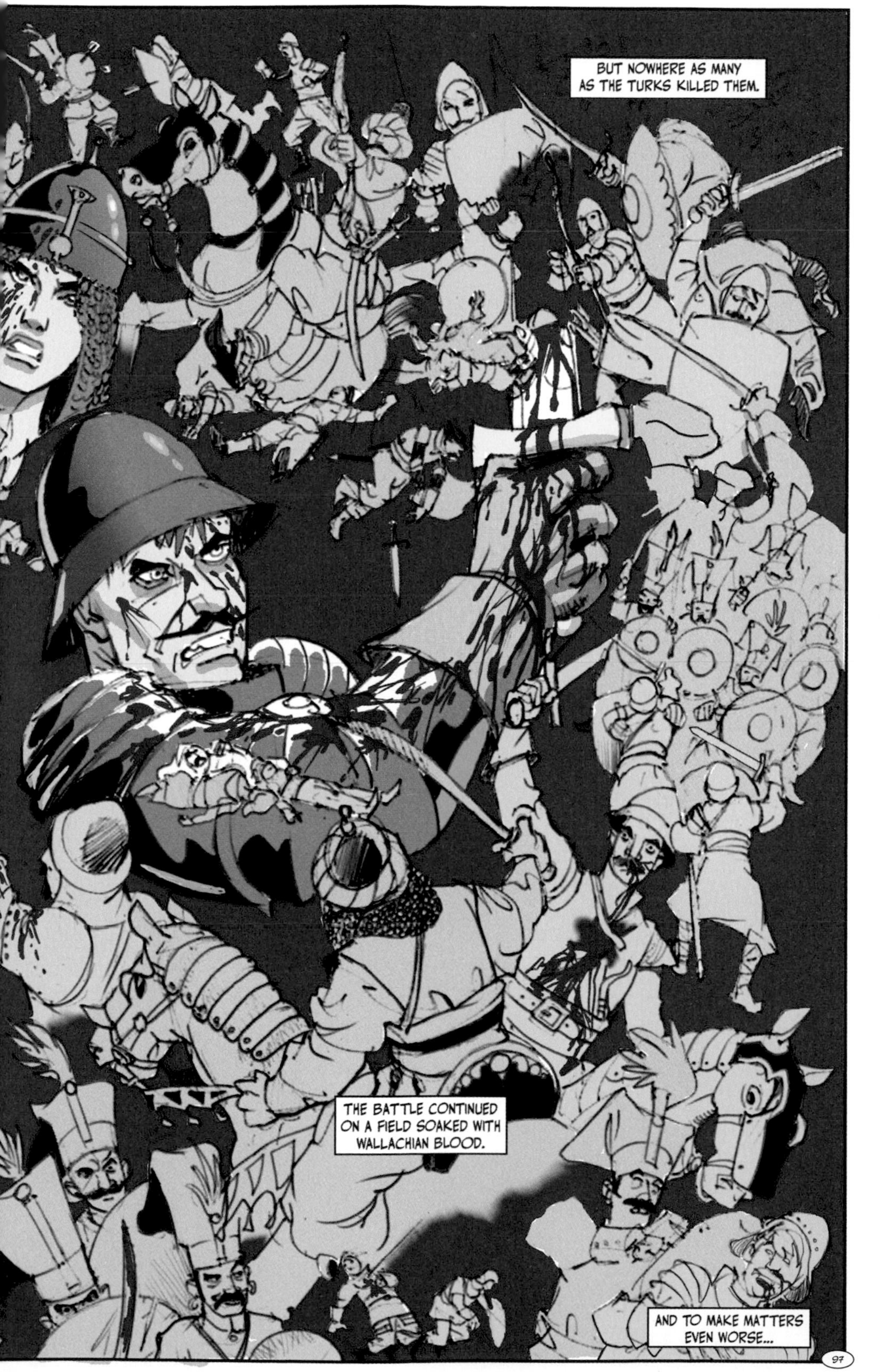
BUT NOWHERE AS MANY AS THE TURKS KILLED THEM.
THE BATTLE CONTINUED ON A FIELD SOAKED WITH WALLACHIAN BLOOD.
AND TO MAKE MATTERS EVEN WORSE...

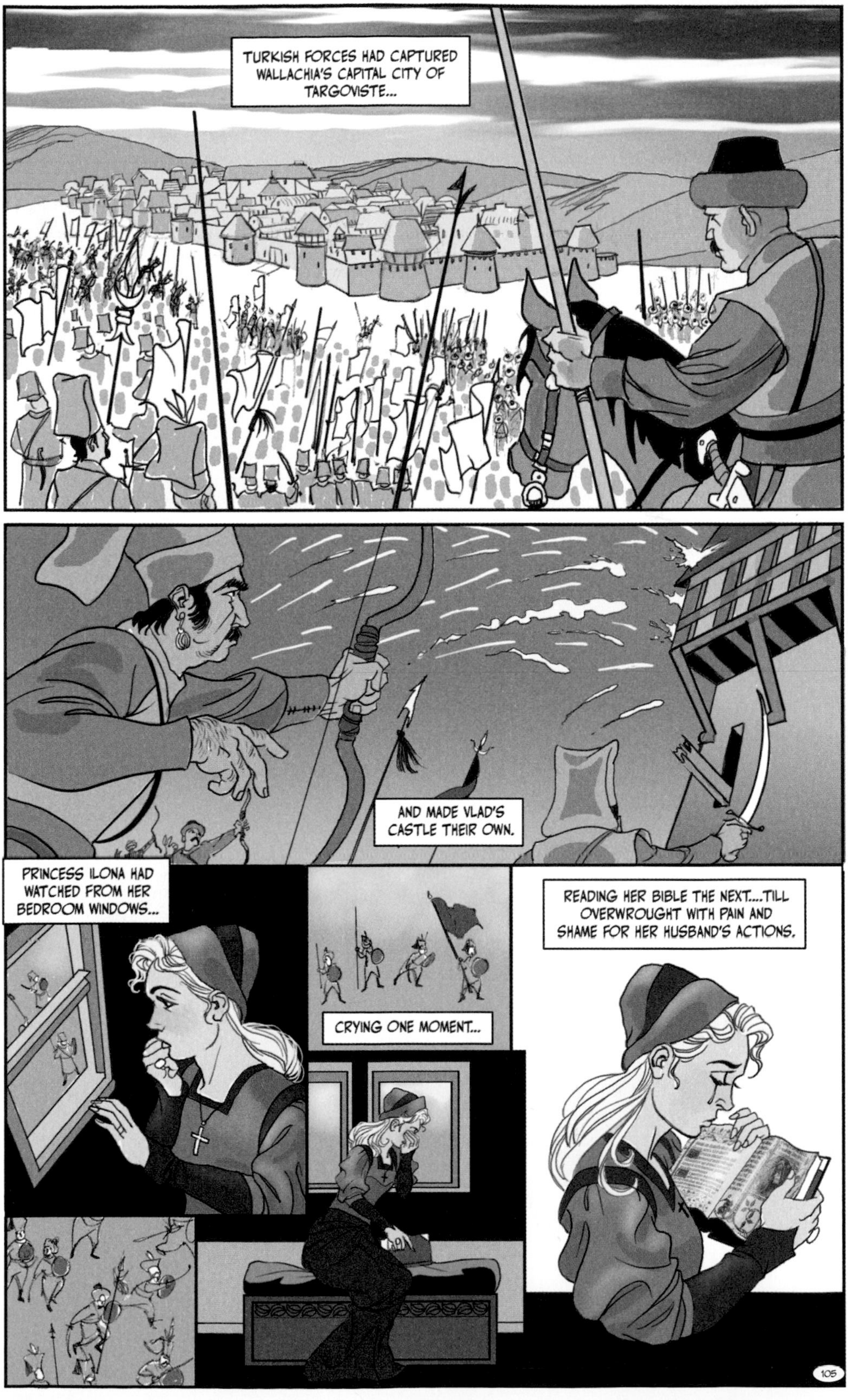
TURKISH FORCES HAD CAPTURED WALLACHIA'S CAPITAL CITY OF TARGOVISTE...
AND MADE VLAD'S CASTLE THEIR OWN.
PRINCESS ILONA HAD WATCHED FROM HER BEDROOM WINDOWS...
CRYING ONE MOMENT...
READING HER BIBLE THE NEXT....TILL OVERWROUGHT WITH PAIN AND SHAME FOR HER HUSBAND'S ACTIONS.

CHAPTER 7: *REVELATION*

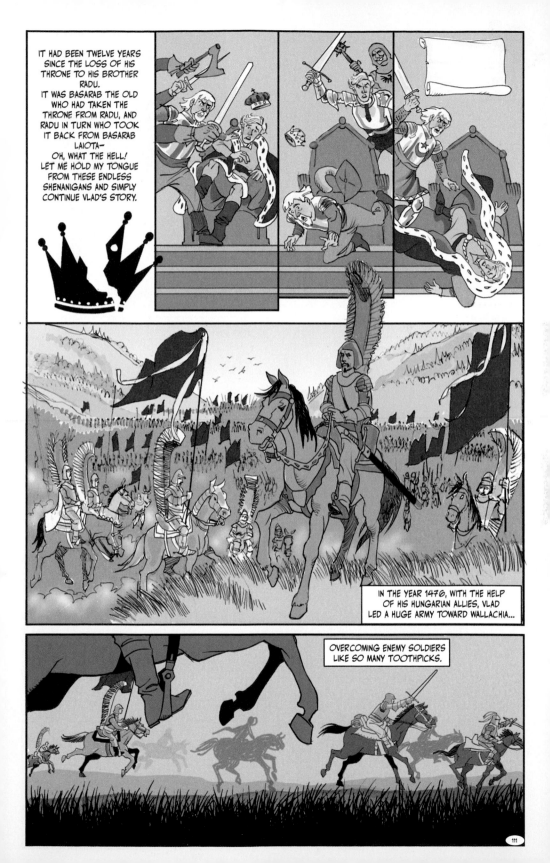

IT HAD BEEN TWELVE YEARS SINCE THE LOSS OF HIS THRONE TO HIS BROTHER RADU.
IT WAS BASARAB THE OLD WHO HAD TAKEN THE THRONE FROM RADU, AND RADU IN TURN WHO TOOK IT BACK FROM BASARAB LAIOTA—
OH, WHAT THE HELL! LET ME HOLD MY TONGUE FROM THESE ENDLESS SHENANIGANS AND SIMPLY CONTINUE VLAD'S STORY.

IN THE YEAR 1476, WITH THE HELP OF HIS HUNGARIAN ALLIES, VLAD LED A HUGE ARMY TOWARD WALLACHIA...

OVERCOMING ENEMY SOLDIERS LIKE SO MANY TOOTHPICKS.

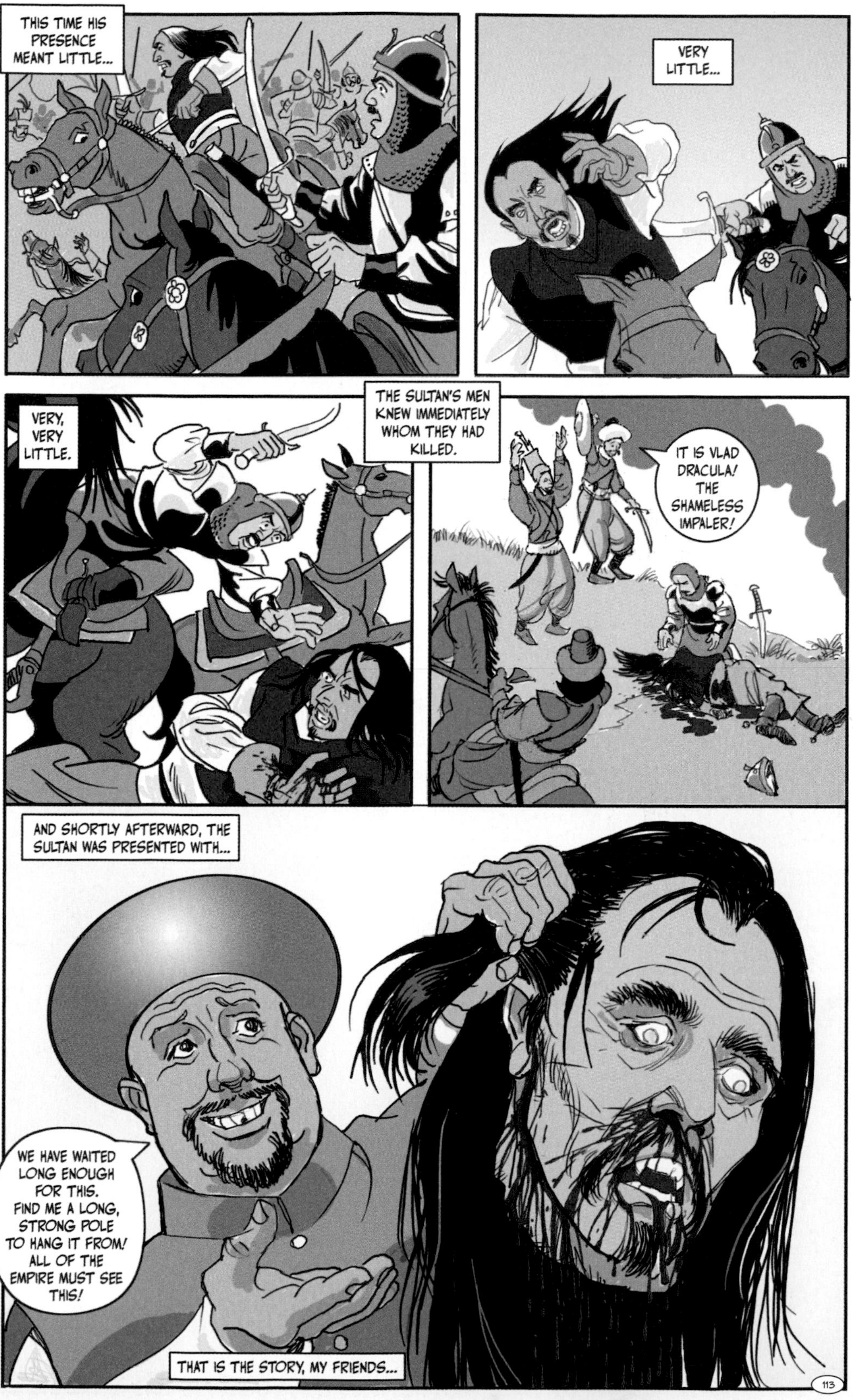
THIS TIME HIS PRESENCE MEANT LITTLE...
VERY LITTLE...
VERY, VERY LITTLE.
THE SULTAN'S MEN KNEW IMMEDIATELY WHOM THEY HAD KILLED.
IT IS VLAD DRACULA! THE SHAMELESS IMPALER!
AND SHORTLY AFTERWARD, THE SULTAN WAS PRESENTED WITH...
WE HAVE WAITED LONG ENOUGH FOR THIS. FIND ME A LONG, STRONG POLE TO HANG IT FROM! ALL OF THE EMPIRE MUST SEE THIS!
THAT IS THE STORY, MY FRIENDS...

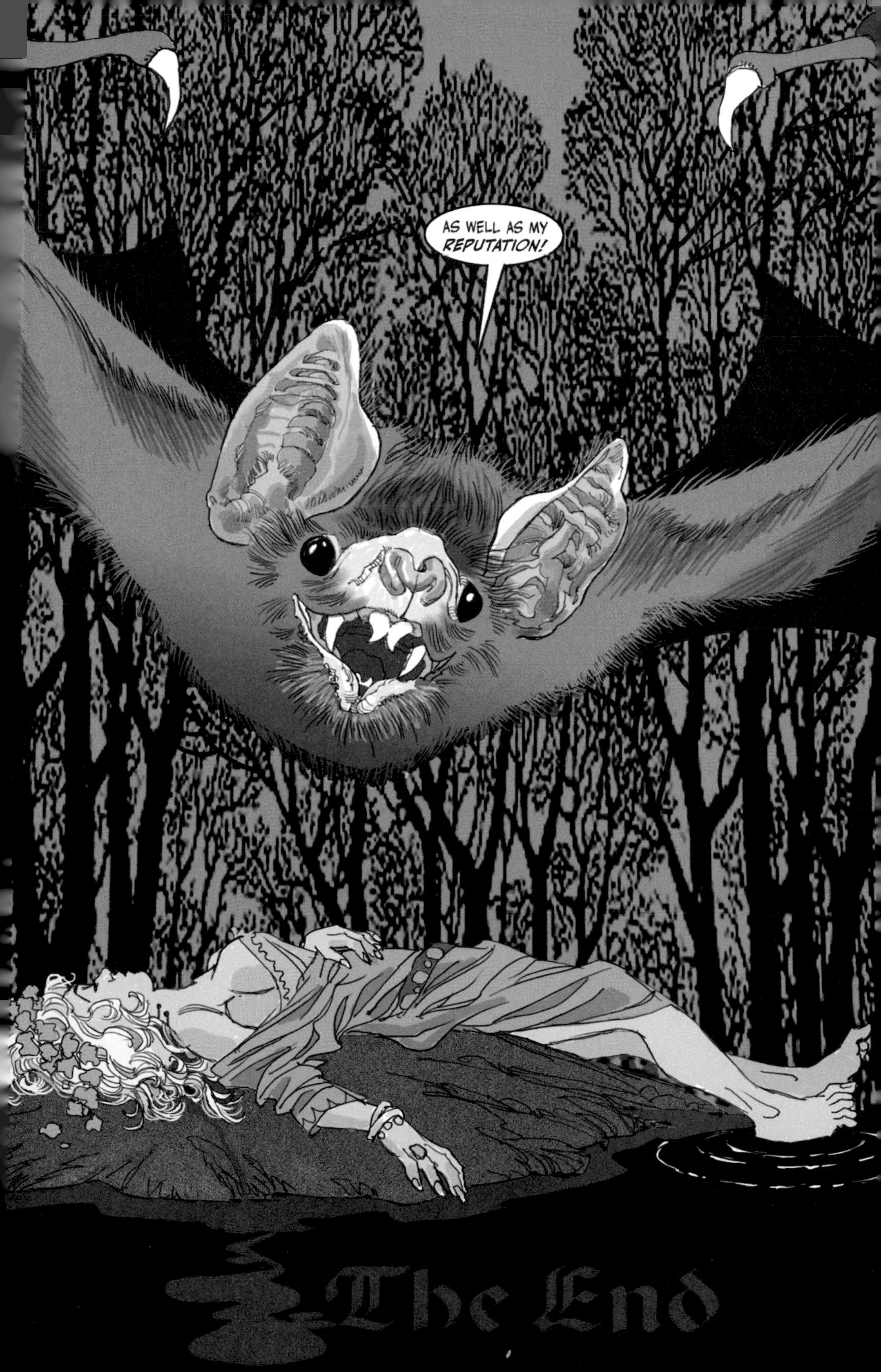
AS WELL AS MY REPUTATION!
The End